Bleak House; Or Poor Jo: A Drama In Four Acts

Charles Dickens

Printing Statement:

Due to the very old age and scarcity of this book, many of the pages may be hard to read due to the blurring of the original text, possible missing pages, missing text, dark backgrounds and other issues beyond our control.

Because this is such an important and rare work, we believe it is best to reproduce this book regardless of its original condition.

Thank you for your understanding.

BLEAK HOUSE; OR, POOR "JO."
A DRAMA, IN FOUR ACTS.
ADAPTED FROM CHARLES DICKENS'S CELEBRATED NOVEL OF "BLEAK HOUSE," BY GEORGE LANDER.

Dramatis Personæ.
First performed at the Pavilion Theatre, Monday, March, 27, 1876.

[See page 13.

SIR LEICESTER DEDLOCK.—"When he has nothing else better to do, he can always contemplate his own greatness." ... Mr. Morrison.
BUCKET.—The Detective, "a stoutly-built, steady-looking, sharp-eyed man in black." Mr. F. Thomas.
MR. TULKINGHORN.—"A Reservoir of family confidences." ... Mr. George Yates.
GUPPY.—"The Young Man of the name of 'Guppy.'" ... Mr. Arthur Williams.
MR. SNAGSBY.—"A mild, bald, timid man, with a shining head, who tends to weakness and obesity." ... Mr. Henry Lynn.
FOOTMAN.—"The Mercury in Powder." Mr. James.
POLICEMAN ... Mr. Johnson.
CORONER ... Mr. Clifton.

JO. (a Crossing-sweeper).—"Very muddy, very ragged, no father, no mother, no friends, knows a broom's a broom, and that it's wicked to tell a lie." ... Mr. J. B. Howe.
GRANDFATHER SMALLWEED ... Mr. Chappell.
THE REV. MR. CHADBAND.—"A toiler and moiler —a consuming vessel." ... Mr. English.
LADY DEDLOCK.—"Beautiful, elegant, accomplished, but with a weariness of soul." Miss M. Foster.
ESTHER SUMMERSON.—"A supposed orphan." Miss H. Wolff.
MRS. SNAGSBY.—"Rumour says that she is jealous and inquisitive." ... Miss L. Reynolds.
MADEMOISELLE HORTENSE.—"A Frenchwoman of two-and-thirty, with something indefinably keen about her anatomy, a very neat she-wolf, imperfectly tamed." ... Miss Harriet Clifton.

No. 388, Dicks' Standard Plays.

COSTUME.

SIR LEICESTER DEDLOCK.—Black frock coat of faultless cut, white vest, drab trousers, black satin stock, high collar, studs in shirt front, long cuffs, reaching nearly to the knuckles, square-toed boots, chain and seals, diamond ring.

MR. TULKINGHORN.—Rusty suit of black—old fashioned swallow-tailed coat, with a high and deep collar and narrow sleeves, single-breasted vest without a collar, and buttoning high up, knee-breeches, tied at the knees with black ribbons, rusty black silk or woollen stockings "they never shine," or gaiters, (in the plates of the novel he is represented as wearing black trousers, which is not in harmony with Dickens's description of him); a wisp of neckcloth (white) round his throat, shoes with steel buckles, heavy old-fashioned chain and seals, old-fashioned high hat, gloves.

BUCKET.—An ample frock-great-coat, closely buttoned up, and with side pockets, black trousers, rather tight, high collar, coloured neckerchief, stout boots, moderately high hat, carries a stout cane with silver top.

GUPPY.—The get-up of a "gent" of the period (1851), short cut-away coat with side pockets, single-breasted flowered vest, with a wide collar, and about three buttons, trousers of a pronounced broad-check pattern, cut at the bottoms to fall over the boots, stick-up collar, and showy neckerchief tied in a bow, a very shiny tall black hat with a narrow brim, short cane with handle, lilac kid gloves, immense ring, and showy watch-chain.

CHADBAND.—Rusty black suit—swallow-tailed coat, rather too large for him, trousers narrow all the way down, low shoes, showing dirty white stockings, dirty white cotton gloves, large black cotton umbrella, a kind of clerical hat.

SNAGSBY.—Grey cut-away coat, rather high in the collar and loose in the nape of the neck, faded flowered or plaid vest, tightish drab trousers, that ride up a little over his boots, neckerchief tied in a small bow, high collar, hat with narrow brim, silver watch and chain.

SMALLWEED.—Rusty black suit—old-fashioned long swallow-tailed coat, too long in the sleeves and too large in the collar, buttoned closely up, very tight trousers, shoes, and dirty white stockings, a high collar, and a black stock, a very high hat, black cloth gloves, crutch stick.

CORONER.—Black suit.

MERCURY IN POWDER.—Gorgeous livery.

JO.—In the plates of the novel he is represented in trousers out at the knees, &c., an old tattered coat, fastened over the chest with one button or a piece of string, no vest, a ragged shirt, a battered little billy-cock hat, with scarcely a bit of brim left, and torn in the crown, dilapidated shoes, and a stump of a broom. On the stage it is customary for effect to dress the part thus:—Ragged shirt and trousers, breast exposed, and bare feet.

LADY DEDLOCK.—In Act 1 a very rich and elegant coloured silk dress, full in the skirt, with a lace shawl thrown over the shoulders, jewelled gold band for front of hair, bracelets, costly rings, watch and chain. In Act 2, a long black cloak, black bonnet and veil, and gloves. In Scene 1, Act 4, same dress worn in Act 1, or a change. In Scene 3, Act 4, wretched and travel-stained dark garments, no hat or bonnet, hair dishevelled and streaming over her shoulders.

ESTHER SUMMERSON.—Blue or grey dress, full behind, neat collar and cuffs, neat little bonnet and cloak for walking dress, gloves and parasol.

MRS. SNAGSBY.—Dress of shot-silk or figured cotton, cap with flowers and long ribbons streaming down. Two large curls at the side of the face.

HORTENSE.—Black dress, fitting well to the figure. Tasty French cap, but not too large, brownish complexion, and smooth dark brown hair. In Act 4, the same dress, cloak and hat worn by Lady Dedlock in Act 2.

For further details as to costumes, &c., and the various make-ups, a reference to the novel, and the plates by Phiz, may be advisable. (See the edition of the novel published in 1853.)

STAGE DIRECTIONS.

EXITS AND ENTRANCES.—R. means *Right*; L. *Left*; D. F. *Door in Flat*; R. D. *Right Door*; L. D. *Left Door*; S. E. *Second Entrance*; U. E. *Upper Entrance*; M. D. *Middle Door*; L. U. E. *Left Upper Entrance*; R. U. E. *Right Upper Entrance*; L. S. E. *Left Second Entrance*; P. S. *Prompt Side*; O. P. *Opposite Prompt*. The particular Entrance, is, in this drama, frequently indicated by a figure, instead of a letter.

RELATIVE POSITIONS.—R. means *Right*; L. *Left*; C. *Centre*; R. C. *Right of Centre*; L. C. *Left of Centre*.

R   RC   C.   LC.   L.

*** *The Reader is supposed to be on the Stage facing the Audience.*

BLEAK HOUSE; OR, POOR "JO."

ACT I.

SCENE I.—*Snagsby's Office in Cook's Court, (1st Grooves).—Flats painted to present the appearance of an office. Door in flat.*

Enter SNAGSBY, *worried*, L.

Snags. What a plague it is to be a law writer. Such a business never was before; stuck on a stool all day long waiting for things to come in, and nothing comes, and then when one is about to knock off, tired of doing nothing, in comes a heap. I'm worrited to death; what with the worry of business, and the nag—nag—nag of my little woman all day long. Her tongue goes just like the clapper of a mill.

Mrs. S. (*Off* L.) Snagsby! Snagsby!

Snags. I'm just having a mouthful of fresh air at the door, my dear. Dear! dear! what a life I do have with my little woman. She won't let me do anything without she knows it.

(*Goes to door, opens it, and admits* MR. TULKINGHORN.)

Snags. Dear me!—Mr. Tulkinghorn!

Mr. T. I want half a word with you, Snagsby.

Snags. With pleasure, sir.

Mr. T. You copied some affidavits for me in the cause of Jarndyce and Jarndyce lately.

Snags. I did.

Mr. T. (*Showing affidavit.*) I want to ask you if you know who copied this.

Snags. (*Looking at it.*) Oh, yes, sir; this was given out to a writer who resides on the opposite side of the lane.

Mr. T. What do you call him?

Snags. We always called him "Nemo," sir.

Mr. T. (*Musing.*) "Nemo"—umph!—that is Latin for no one.

Snags. He was only a casual hand, sir.

Mr. T. Have you ever given this man work before?

Snags. Oh dear yes, sir.

Mr. T. Where does he live?

Snags. Ahem!—he did live, sir, at a wretched place—a rag and bottle shop kept by a man named Krook.

Mr. T. But where does he live now?

Snags. Ahem!—He doesn't live at all, sir—he is dead.

Mr. T. Dead. Oh! when did he die?

Snags. Yesterday, sir. Died very sudden, I believe—it is supposed from the effects of opium, which he was in the habit of taking in large quantities. Ahem!

Mr. T. Dear! dear! I should like to get some particulars about the man. Do you know anything about him?

Snags. I assure you, sir, that I know no more where he came from than——

Mr. T. Where he has gone to, I suppose, though that perhaps might be guessed.

Snags. Perhaps the inquest may bring out something, sir.

Mr. T. Perhaps it may. Where, and when, is it held?

Snags. This very evening, at six o'clock, at the Sol's Arms, close by.

Mr. T. It is that now. If you can spare time we will go and hear it.

Snags. With pleasure, sir — with pleasure. (*Aside.*) Whatever will my little woman say?

Mr. T. I say, Snagsby, not a word to your little woman.

Snags. Oh, dear me, sir, not a word, sir—not a word.

Enter MRS. SNAGSBY, L. *she curtseys to Mr. T., who nods to her.*

Mr. T. I'll wait for you in the court, Snagsby.

Mrs. S. There, I'm snubbed, and all through you. You don't make enough of your wife before customers. Such a little treasure as I am.

Snags. My dear, business is business, and there is a time and place for everything.

Mrs. S. (*Taking his hat off.*) Where are you going?

Snags. To the inquest on "Nemo," my dear, with Mr. Tulkinghorn.

Mrs. S. What is all this mystery about? Come, sir.

Snags. My dear, there is no mystery—give me my hat. Mr. Tulkinghorn is waiting. (*Moves towards door.*) Come, my dear.

(*Mrs Snagsby gets his hat from* L.)

Mrs. S. (*Getting between him and the door, and holding the hat behind her.*) If you attempt to keep any secrets from me, you shall suffer for it. Ah! you may look, but I have had my ear to the keyhole all the time. I know (*mimicking him.*) "Not a word to your little woman." "Oh, dear me, sir, not a word, sir—not a word." (*Puts the hat on his head.*) Now go, sir, but beware and not keep any secrets from me. (*Stands and points to the open door. Snagsby goes out nervously.*) If I were inquisitive, I shouldn't mind; but there is not a spark of inquisitiveness in my disposition. Oh, dear me, no. [*Exit*, L.

SCENE II.—*Room at the Sol's Arms,—(2nd Grooves.)—An old fashioned brown wainscoted parlour. Sporting pictures on walls—door* R. C.—CORONER *and* JURY *assembled at table up stage.* L.—*the Coroner, at opening of scene, busily engaged writing.* TULKINGHORN *seated to* L. *of Coroner—*SNAGSBY *with lookers on, women amongst them, grouped near door—*LANDLORD *in striped sleeved waistcoat (old style) a prominent figure in the group. Foolscap paper on table—pens and ink—lighted candles.* BEADLE *at door, very pompous—subdued conversation amongst lookers on at opening.*

Bea. Now then—silence there—silence!—not so much talk.

Cor. (*To Jury.*) Well, Gentlemen, you are empannelled here to inquire into the death of a certain man known commonly by the name of "Nemo." Evidence has been given before you of the circumstances attending that death, and you will give your verdict according to the evidence. (*A loud crash, as if skittles were being played.*) Whatever's that?

Bea. It's skittles, sir. It's not a bit of use talking to 'em. I says: "There's a hinquest being held," and they says: "Blow the hinquest!"

Cor. (*To Landlord.*) Do stop it, Landlord, while this is going on. [*Exit landlord.*
Really it is disgraceful that Coroner's Courts should be held in pot-houses. (*One of the Jury whispers to Coroner.*) I hear that there is a crossing sweeper boy waiting outside, who knew the deceased—Suppose we hear what he has got to say, he may enlighten us a little, perhaps. Let him be brought forward.

[*Exit Beadle.*
(*Tulkinghorn converses with Coroner.*)

Enter BEADLE, *with* JO.

(*Exclamations of pity at Jo's wretched appearance as Beadle leads him down* R.)

Bea. Stand there, boy. Order there! silence!
(*When Jo has got into his position, the Beadle suddenly claps a small bible right under his nose, to swear him, holding it at arm's length.*)

Bea. (*Gabbling the words.*) You shall swear to speak the truth—the whole truth—and nothing but the truth. (*Jo is astonished.*)

Cor. Never mind that. Now, boy—what's your name?

Jo. Jo, sir.

Cor. Jo what?

Jo. Don't know, sir.

Cor. Not know your name!

Jo. No, sir—wish I did.

Cor. Nonsense! you must know your other name. You have got another name besides Jo.

Jo. I've got a nickname, sir.

Cor. What's that?

Jo. Toughy, sir.

Cor. Pshaw! Don't you know that everybody has two names?

Jo. No, sir—never heerd of such a thing.

Cor. Where were you christened?

Jo. What, sir?

Cor. Christened—given a name and sprinkled with holy water.

Jo. I've often been splashed with muddy water, sir.

Cor. I want none of that. Don't you know that Jo is short for a longer name?

Jo. Long enough for me, sir; I don't find no fault with it.

Cor. Spell it.

Jo. Can't, sir.

Cor. Where, and who are your parents?

Jo. Never had any, sir.

Cor. Amusing young rascal this. Come!—no more of this nonsense! Who were your father and mother?

Jo. Don't know. Parish is father, and a hard one too. Charity is mother, and a stingy old gal she is, I can tell you.

Cor. Where were you brought up?

Jo. Brought up, did yer say?—generally by the perlice—been brought up twice afore the beak.

Cor. What for?

Jo. For not a movin' on.

Cor. Been to school?

Jo. Lor! no, sir.

Cor. Where's your home?

Jo. What's "home," sir?

Cor. Don't you know what home is?

Jo. I knows a broom's a broom, and knows it's wicked to tell a lie, that's all I knows.

Cor. Who told you that?—Come!

Jo. I don't know—I knows nothink, I don't.

Cor. Do you know what will be done to you i[n] the next world if you tell a lie to these gentleme[n] here?

Jo. Not 'xactly, but something wery bad arte[r] I'm dead—and serve me right if I told a lie.

Cor. Tell us what you knew about the deceased[.]

Jo. I don't know anythink—except that he w[as] wery good to me—and when I see him lyin' [a] stretched out just now, I wished he could ha[ve] heard me tell him so. He was wery good to m[e] he was.

Cor. He must have talked to you, and told yo[u] something about himself.

Jo. I don't know nothink, I tell you. I ain't [a] goin' to show him up now he's dead.

Cor. Stand aside. The boy's an idiot. H[is] evidence is worthless. It is no use swearing o[ne] who is next door to a heathen.

(*Beadle puts Jo aside. Snagsby wor[ks] his way round to Jo.*)

Jo. He was wery good to me, he was.

Cor. Well, gentlemen. Here's a man unknow[n] proved to have been in the habit of taking opi[um] in large quantities for a year and a half, fou[nd] dead of too much opium. If you think you h[ave] any evidence to lead you to the conclusion that [he] committed suicide you must come to that c[on-]clusion.—If you think it a case of accidental dea[th] you will come to a verdict accordingly. (*The J[ury] confer. Foreman whispers to Coroner.*) Ah! j[ust] so, "Accidental death," quite right, a pro[per] verdict. Gentlemen you are discharged.

[*Exeunt all but Jo and Snag[sby.*

Snags. Jo—Hi!—Toughy!—Hi—(*Nudging [him]*) Jo, here's half a crown for you. No thank[s,] never mind. If ever you see me coming past y[our] crossing with my little woman, don't allude t[o it,] or she'll blow me up.

Jo. Oh, sir,—no, sir.

Snags. (*At door.*) Poor little beggar!

Jo. I know what I'll do. His grave'll be v[ery] plain, it will. I'll buy a flower or two, and a b[ox—]box—somethink that lives in winter. I can g[et it] in the market—and I'll plant it on his grave, I [will,] arter he's buried, an' I know it won't die for [want] of, my tears to water it. Ah! he was wery goo[d to] me, he was.

(*Closed in slou[gh.*

SCENE III.—*Street near the Sol's Arms.—*[*Enter*] TULKINGHORN *and* SNAGSBY, L.

Snags. Well, sir, we don't seem to have got [any] nearer to it. We are about as wise as we [were] before.

Tulk. (*In reverie.*) Yes.

Snags. It's very aggravatin', sir, when one v[ants] to get at a thing and can't.—Lor! if my [old] woman wanted to find anything out and cou[ldn't,] she'd be in such a fever.

Tulk. Your little woman, Snagsby, has the usual ailing of her sex: she wants to know everybody's business.

Snags. That's about it, sir. Paul Pry was a fool to her.

Tulk. I think that boy knew more than he chose to say.

Snags. Perhaps so, sir, and perhaps not; but I don't think Mr. "Nemo" was a man to let anybody know much about himself. I don't want to know, sir, but do you think that "Nemo" was a gentleman in disguise, or out of luck?

Tulk. (*Tartly.*) How should I know?

Snags. Of course not, sir. He had very delicate hands, though he generally kept them very dirty, if that was any sign of gentility.

Tulk. Delicate hands!—Ah! so have pickpockets.

Snags. True, sir, though I don't know any pickpockets myself. I don't want to know, sir, but do you think that it is likely to turn out that "Nemo" was the heir to some considerable property, or something of that kind?

Tulk. Don't ask questions.

Snags. Certainly not, sir; but who do you think he was. Thank goodness, I'm not at all inquisitive, like my little woman.

Tulk. Surely, the man must have had some friends in his business who would be likely to know something about him and his antecedents; or he may have known some female, who could give us some information relative to him.

Snags. Well, sir, I don't think he was exactly the sort of man that the fair sex, as a rule, would be likely to take up with; though some of them, as my little woman says, are not at all particular, for that matter, with whom they take up, provided the party wears a pair of trousers. Ahem! But, as regards his connections in a general way, sir, not to put too fine a point on it, if you were to say to me: Snagsby, here's £20,000, I couldn't tell, sir, anything about 'em. All I know is, that about a year and a half ago he came into our place one morning after breakfast, and finding my little woman in the shop, gave her a specimen of his handwriting, and asked for work. My little woman was took by something about him—whether by his being unshaved, or his wanting attention, or by what her ladies' reason, I leave you to judge—and she gave him some work, he giving the name of Nemo, which my little woman always called Nimrod—and so "Nimrod," or "Nemo," gradually got into work at our place, and that is all I know. The other hands said he had sold himself to the—Ahem!—gentleman in black; but I'm sure I don't know.

Tulk. If so, I can only say the gentleman in black was no great gainer by the bargain.

Snags. You are facetious, sir. Ahem!

Tulk. Well, Snagsby, if you should hear of anybody who knew the deceased man, inform me of it.

Snags. Certainly, sir, with the greatest of pleasure. Is there anything else, sir?

Tulk. Nothing at present, Snagsby.

Snags. Thank you, sir, then I'll get home, or my little woman will begin to scold. [*Exit.*

Tulk. Good evening, Snagsby. I think I have got a clue to the dark page in my Lady Dedlock's past life. I am convinced that there was something discreditable in her early career. Her austerity and gloom; her reserve; the peculiar handwriting that I have noticed in several of her most valued books, and which so clearly resembles that of the affidavit that so excited our curiosity; her unexplained visits to town, from time to time; her absolute silence as to her past life; all point to a mystery that I am determined, if possible, to unravel. If I succeed, and find that she is an unworthy and disgraced woman, she shall be cast down from the high place to which Sir Leicester Dedlock's infatuated love has raised her. If all that I suspect is true, she is unworthy of being the wife of so honourable and excellent a man.
[*Exit.*

SCENE IV.—*Long Drawing-room at Chesney Wold. A picturesque Elizabethan room, panelled and hung with tapestry.—Old-fashioned mantelpiece and fireplace,* R.*, and logs burning—long window,* C.*, the frame and bars covered with gauze—terrace backing, and dark, pitchy landscape—the window entirely concealed with a thick curtain, to exclude the limelight that is thrown on the ghostly figure just before the act terminates—carpet down, and rug—hand-table near fireplace, and easy chair—table and easy chair,* L.*—cabinets and antique chairs, and any articles that add to the general sombre effect of the scene—rich covers on tables—books, &c.—lighted lamps on tables—a portrait of a man in armour over mantelpiece—door,* L. 2 E.

SIR LEICESTER DEDLOCK *in chair,* L.*, and* LADY DEDLOCK *in chair,* R.*, discovered, Sir Leicester, with papers before him, Lady Dedlock listlessly turning over the pages of a book.*

Sir L. Well, I do not want to terrify you, or, as you seem so interested in the legend that is connected with the Ghost's Walk (as the terrace outside is called), I would tell it to you.

Lady D. Do, by all means; I have often wished to hear it.

Sir L. You must know, then, that in the days of Charles the First, Sir Morbury Dedlock, one of my ancestors, was on that monarch's side in his struggle with his parliament; but his lady, who had none of the family blood in her veins, was on the side of his enemies, and gave them information. When any of the county gentlemen who favoured the King's cause met here, it is said that she was always nearer to the door of the council-room than they supposed.

Lady D. Ah! feminine curiosity.

Sir L. Precisely. On account of this division between Sir Morbury and his lady, they led a very troubled life, and she hated the family, as the family hated her. When the Dedlocks were about to ride out from Chesney Wold, she is supposed to have gone down into the stables at the dead of night, and lamed their horses. And the story is, that once, at such an hour, her husband saw her gliding down-stairs, and followed her down into the stall where his own horse stood. Then he seized her by the wrist, and in a struggle, or a fall, or by the horse lashing out, she was lamed in the hip, and from that hour began to pine away. What was that? (*Listening.*)

Lady D. (*Contemptuously.*) Nothing. Go on!

Sir L. She never spoke to anyone, or complained of being in pain; but, day after day, she tried to walk upon the terrace, and, with the help of a stick and the stone balustrade, went up and down, up and down, in greater difficulty every day. At last, one afternoon, her husband, to whom she had never on any occasion since the accident opened her lips, saw her, as he was standing by the great south window yonder (*Pointing to window*), drop upon the pavement. He hastened to raise her, but she repulsed him, and, looking fixedly and coldly at him, said, "I will die here, where I have walked; and I will walk here till I am in my grave. I will walk here till the pride of this house is humbled: and, when danger or disgrace is coming to it, let the Dedlocks listen for my step." There and then she died, and from those days the name has come down—"The Ghost's Walk." If the tread is an echo, it is an echo that is heard only after dark. So sure as there is sickness, or death, or disgrace in the family, it is heard then. It is strange, but lately I have sometimes fancied that I heard it.

Lady D. These old legends are intensely interesting.

Sir L. They are.

(*Looks over papers; she resumes her book for a few moments.*)

Lady D. You seem to have an unusual amount of correspondence.

Sir L. Nothing in it—nothing whatever.

Lady D. I think I saw one of Mr. Tulkinghorn's long effusions.

Sir L. He sends—I really beg your pardon—(*Selecting a letter*)—a letter for you. It really slipped my memory. He says——Oh! here I have it! (*Reads.*) "I beg my respectful compliments to my lady, and will you do me the favour to mention, as it may interest her, that I have something to tell her in reference to the person who copied the affidavit in the Chancery suit which so powerfully excited her curiosity. I have seen him."

Lady D. Mr. Tulkinghorn writes as if it were a matter of the most profound importance. I merely thought the handwriting peculiar for a legal document. Mr. Tulkinghorn is troubling himself needlessly.

Enter FOOTMAN, D. 2 E. L.

Ser. (*Announcing grandly.*) Mr. Tulkinghorn.

(*Lady D. resumes book. Sir L. rises to receive Mr. T.*)

Enter MR. TULKINGHORN, D. 2 E. L.

Sir L. (*Warmly.*) How do you do, Mr. Tulkinghorn?

Lady D. (*Stiffly, over book.*) How do you do?

Tulk. Quite well, Sir Leicester; quite well, my lady, I hope you are both well, too.

Sir L. Quite well. (*To Footman.*) A chair.

[*Servant places chair* C., *and exit*, D. 2 E. L.

Tulk. I should have come down sooner, but I have been so engaged in the various Chancery suits that——

Lady D. (*Laughing.*) This dreadful Chancery business wearies me. I will leave you.

(*Rising to go.*)

Sir L. By no means.—Mr. Tulkinghorn and I can talk it over in my study.

Tulk. To be sure we can. By the bye—concerning the handwriting of that affidavit that your ladyship was so anxious about. I inquired about the man, and, what is very strange, I found him——

Lady D. Not to be any out of the way person, I hope?

Tulk. I found him dead.

Lady D. Dear me!

Tulk. I was directed to a miserable poverty-stricken place, and found him dead.

(*Lady D. drops book.*)

Sir L. Excuse me, Mr. Tulkinghorn, I think the less said the better.

(*Picks up book, and returns it to Lady D.*)

Lady D Pray let me hear the story out. How very shocking.

Tulk. Whether by his own hand——

Sir L. Really——

Lady D Now do let me hear the story. Go on, Mr. Tulkinghorn.

Tulk. I was about to say, whether he had died by his own hand or not, it was beyond my power to tell you. The coroner's jury found that he took poison accidentally.

Lady D. And what kind of a man was this deplorable creature?

Tulk. Very difficult to say. He had died so wretchedly, and was so neglected. with his gipsy colour, and his wild black hair, and beard, that I should have considered him the commonest of the common.

Lady D. What did they call the wretched being?

Tulk. They called him what he had called himself, but no one knew his name. He was known as Nemo, which is Latin for no one.

Lady D. And that was the only name he was known by—dear me!—How long pray, had the poor wretch resided at his lodging?

Tulk. About eighteen months.

Lady D. And was there no clue to his antecedents?

Tulk. None.

Lady D. No letters?

Tulk. None.

Lady D. Poor wretch!—What a collection of horrors. Thank you, Mr. Tulkinghorn.

(*Resumes novel.*)

Sir L. I trust, Mr. Tulkinghorn, we shall hear no more of this ghastly story. It is some begging letter impostor with whose handwriting Lady Dedlock is doubtless familiar. Let us retire to my study, and talk over this Chancery business—at least, after you have partaken of some refreshment. Her ladyship will excuse us?

Lady D. Oh! certainly.

[*Exeunt Mr. T. and Sir L. L., the former with a profound bow to Lady D.*

Lady D. (*Rising and coming down.*) What is this terrible story that he has told? Does he know more? Does he know the story of my most wretched and wicked life? His cold, cruel eyes were fixed on mine as if they would have searched into my very brain and read my secret; but I was calm, and baffled him. How the past comes back to me. Could that abandoned, miserable wretch, have been Arthur Hawdon, my first and only love—although the author of my ruin—for many a year dead to me—the father of my child? Oh! what a dreadful retribution for sin like ours, that he should die like that, and I should live to hear the story.

Enter FOOTMAN, D. L. 2 E.

Foot. If you please, your ladyship, a young man of the name of Guppy!

Lady D. Guppy!—Guppy!

Foot. He says he wrote for an interview.

Lady D. Oh! ah!—admit him. (*Footman stares.*) Admit him.

[*Exit Footman, and re-enter showing in GUPPY. Footman shows great contempt for Guppy, and exits*, D. L. 2 E. *Guppy very nervous, stands near door, brushing his hat with his coat sleeve, and bowing.*

Lady D. (*After a pause.*) You are the person, I

think, who wrote me all those letters stating that you had something of the greatest importance to communicate. Your name is—is Puppy.

Gup. No, Guppy, your ladyship, Guppy—(*Conceitedly*) Guppy, of the firm of Kenge and Carboy, Linkin's Inn.

Lady D. You have been most importunate, sir. I had no desire to see you, but, as you have come, what have you to say to me?

Gup. Thank your ladyship. I am going to speak to you in the strictest confidence, I hope; because if your ladyship were to split on me to my employers, I should get the bullet.

Lady D. The what?

Gup. The sack, I mean—I beg your ladyship's pardon—I mean, discharged. (*Approaches her confidentially.*) I am not aware if your ladyship ever happened to hear of a young lady of the name of Esther Summerson.

Lady D. Yes, I have. She resides near us with her guardian. I have a great regard for her.

Gup. (*Getting a little closer.*) Do you think she is like your ladyship's family?

Lady D. (*Coldly.*) No.

Gup. Now, I do. She is the image of your ladyship, and there's a mystery about her bringing up —I mention it in confidence—which I've heard of at Kenge and Carboy's in the way of my profession. Now, you must know your ladyship, that Miss Summerson's image is imprinted on my 'art, and if I could prove that she was in any way related to your ladyship—which would give her a right to be made a party to the great Chancery suit of Jarndyce and Jarndyce, why I might make Miss Summerson more disposed to favour my suit than she is at present, and become Mrs. G. eventually.

Lady D. (*Languidly.*) Ah! Indeed!

Gup. (*Very much emboldened, and leaning over table.*) Did your ladyship ever know a Miss Barbary—the lady who brought up Miss Summerson?

Lady D. (*Agitated.*) N—no—Stay—I think so. Yes, yes.

Gup. Very good, so far. Was Miss B. ever connected with your ladyship's family? (*Lady D. shakes her head.*) Not to your ladyship's knowledge, but she might be, wery good. Now I have a witness —a party who was servant to this here Miss Barbary, and one day Miss Barbary let out to her that the little gal's name was not Esther Summerson, but Esther Hawdon.

Lady D. Great heaven!

Gup. Wery good again. Now another pint is this: your ladyship may have read in the papers of the death of a law writer in great distress, at the house of an old party of the name of Krook, near Chancery Lane.

Lady D. I have heard the story.

Gup. Wery good—just so. Now, I have found out the right name of that deceased indiwiddle. His name was Hawdon.

Lady D. (*With forced calmness.*) Well, Mr. Guppy, what of that?

Gup. Hold hard, your ladyship, I'm comin' gradually to the pint. He left a bundle of old letters behind him, which his landlord, who has since died of internal combustion through the rum in his stummick catching fire, got hold of, but which to-morrow will be in my possession.

Lady D. What—what of that?

Gup. I'm a comin' to the pint, my lady. I want to know whether there isn't enough in all this to justify your ladyship going further into the case. Would your ladyship not like to have those letters?

Lady D. You may bring them if you choose.

Gup. Wery good. Your ladyship shall have them. I wish your ladyship a wery respectful adoo!—adoo!—adoo! (*Going.*)

Lady D. (*Taking out purse.*) Stay.

Gup. Oh dear, no—thank your ladyship, I'm not a hextortioner. I'm a gent in my feelin's, and in all my hactions. Keep your gold. My only hobject is to serve Miss Esther Summerson—the hidol of my 'art. Adoo! your ladyship, adoo!— once more adoo!

[*Makes a profound bow, and exits,* D. L. 2 E.

Lady D. (*With a passionate cry and coming c.*) O, my child!—my child!—Not dead in the first hours of her life, as my cruel sister told me, but sternly nurtured by her after she had renounced me and mine. Bear up, my heart! and Heaven,—give me strength to hide its passions! Oh! what a wretched creature I am—envied by those who, if they knew what was beneath the mask I wear, would loathe and shun me. Two things I have heard to-night: his wretched life and death, and that my daughter lives. The ghostly legend is true: when calamity or death is coming to the house of Dedlock, the phantom of its ancestress walks. I have heard its ghostly step upon the terrace, and knew it walked for me. I feel its baneful influence about me—Air! air!

(*She hurries with faltering step to the window, and draws the curtains, revealing a ghostly female figure, costumed in the fashion of King Charles the First's time, standing on the terrace, with its gaze directed full upon her, and the forefinger of its right hand pointed menacingly at her; the left hand rests on a crutch stick. The face of the figure is stern and forbidding. The lime light is full on the figure. As Lady Dedlock glimpses the figure, she drops the curtains, and utters a loud shriek of terror, falling prostrate; or she may be caught in the arms of* SIR LEICESTER DEDLOCK, *as he and* MR. TULKINGHORN *come on at her shriek.—Act drop quick.*)

END OF ACT I.

ACT II.

SCENE I.—*A street, with Jo's crossing.* 1st. Groove.

TWO MEN cross, L. to R. *Jo follows and begs.*

Jo. Please give a copper to poor Jo. (*Is repulsed —the men exit,* R.) Not a copper, and they all uses my crossin'. I'm starvin, I am, and can't get a penny. I feel as if I could sit down and have a good cry.

Enter LADY DEDLOCK, *dressed in black, and veiled* L. *Jo precedes her, sweeping and begging.*

Jo. Please give a copper to a poor boy, mum. I'm very hungry.

(*Lady D. crosses to* R., *and being much importuned by Jo, stops, and looks at him intently.*)

Lady D. Are you the boy I read of in the papers?

Jo. (*Suspiciously and drawing back.*) I don't know nothing about no papers. I don't know nothing about no papers at all.

Lady D. Were you examined at an inquest?

Jo. Oh! where I was took by the beadle, you mean. Was the boy's name at the inkwich, Jo?

Lady D. Yes.

Jo. Oh! that's me.

Lady D. Do not be afraid to speak to me. You knew the——the——

Jo. You mean about the man—him as was dead.

Lady D. Hush! Speak in a whisper—Yes. Did he look when he was living so very ill and poor?

Jo. Oh! jist——

Lady D. Did he look——Oh! not like you?

Jo. Not so bad as me, I'm a reg'lar one, I am. You didn't know him, did you?

Lady D. How dare you ask me if I knew him?

Jo. No offence, my lady.

Lady D. How dare you call me a lady, I'm not a lady; I'm a servant.

Jo. You—Oh! you are a jolly servant.

Lady D. Listen, and be silent. Don't talk to me, and stand further from me. Can you show me all those places that were spoken of in the account I read: the place he wrote for, the place he died at, and the place that you were taken to, and the place where he was buried? Go before, and show me all those places. Point out the places; but don't speak to me, unless I do to you. Don't look back. Do what I want, and I will pay you well.

Jo. I'm fly, but fen larks you know, stow hooking it.

Lady D. I don't understand you. Go before, and I will give you more money than ever you had in your life.

[*Jo goes off,* R., *she following—both slowly.*

SCENE II.—*The Burial Ground—very dilapidated and neglected,—(4th Grooves.) Iron railings, fixed on brickwork, and gate, with two broken steps—a dismal light in a lamp above the gate—through the railings a few neglected graves and broken tombstones are seen—the backing of the churchyard shows the backs of houses of a mean sort, in some of the windows of which there is a dim light. The scene must in its entirety impress the audience by its dreary aspect. If the churchyard is made "pretty" the desired impression will fail to be conveyed. (Double limelight on.)*

Enter JO, *preceding* LADY DEDLOCK, L.

Lady D. (*As Jo pauses.*) Who lives there?

Jo. Him what give him his writing to do, and give me half a bull.

Lady D. (*After looking where Jo points.*) Go on to the next. (*Jo pauses.*) Who lives here?

Jo. He lived here.

Lady D. In which room?

Jo. In the back room, there. You can see the room from here, up there, that's where I saw him stretched out. Over there was the public-house where I was took to. He was wery good to me, he was, and often used to give me a supper when I hadn't got one. When I see him all stretched out at the inkwich I wished he could have heerd me tell 'em how wery good to me he was.

Lady D. Tell me all you know.

Jo. I only know as how he was wery neglected and unhappy, and had no friend but me in the world to speak to. I knows as he was hooted in the streets by the boys as if he was a savage what ate children, instead o' givin 'em hapenies, as he did.

Lady D. How came you to know him?

Jo. I'll tell yer. It was one wet night, when I was shiverin' in a doorway near my crossin', he stopped and spoke to me, and asked me if I had any friends. I told him, none. "No more have I," says he. And I saw his eyes full of tears, an' he was cryin'. "Have you nowhere to sleep?" says he, an' I says, "no." "An' no supper?"—"No," says I. With that he give me the price of a bed, an' a night's lodgin'. Arter that we soon got to know each other.

Lady D. Go on, pray.

Jo. When he had no money, an' I had none, he used for to say, "Jo, I am as poor as you are to-day;" but when he had money and I had none, he always give me some; and when I had it, and he had none, I always give some to him.

Lady D. Did he ever tell you anything about himself? did he ever mention any names?

Jo. No, only he once said, I rec'lect, as he had been a gentleman and a hossifer. If he was ever a hossifer, it was in a wery ragged regiment—that's all I knows. I think he was a larkin' with me.

Lady D. Where was he buried?

Jo. (*Pointing to churchyard.*) He was put there.

Lady D. Where?

Jo. There.

Lady D. (*Going to gate.*) What a scene of horror!

Jo. (*At gate, and pointing through it as he kneels.*) There—over yonder, among them pile o' bones, an' close to the kitchen window o' them houses. They put him wery nigh the top. They was obliged to stamp on the coffin to get it in. I could unkiver it for you with my broom if the gate was open. That's why they locks it I suppose. It's always locked. Look at the rat!—Hi!—Look! There he goes, into the ground. Hullo!

Lady D. (*Horrified.*) Is this place of abomination consecrated ground?

Jo. I don't know nothink about *consequential* ground.

Lady D. Is it blessed?

Jo. (*With vacant stare.*) Which? I'm blessed if I know, but I should think it warn't. Blessed! —it ain't done much good if it was. Blessed!—I should think it was bothered, myself. But I don't know nothink. (*Gets down stage.*)

Lady D. (*Kneeling on steps and looking through the gate.*) O my first and only love, is it there you lie in that vile pauper's grave, so dead—so dead to me. To think that he, who was once a gentleman, should come to so miserable and degraded an end. If, for my wrongs, I wanted revenge, in this sight there would be more than I, or anyone, however great their wrongs, could need. (*Gives a last look at the grave, and comes to Jo, who is watching her, and gives him money.*) There. Thanks! and God bless you! Show me the grave again.

[*Jo again goes to gate and points out grave. She steals off,* R.

Jo. (*Missing her as he turns round.*) I don't see her nowhere. She's hooked it. (*Looks at money.*) What's this? Gold! A sovereign! I never had sich a thing afore in my hand in all the born days o' my life. (*Several roughs watch him,* R. *as he toys with money.*) This is a hadwenture. She must be a real lady, though. I wonder, if I was dead, if anybody would make a sovereign out o' me. Not they, I don't think they'd make a bob, or even a copper, unless it was out o' my old rags. And yet, I'd rather he was here, than I'd have a hatful o' yaller ones like this.

(*Roughs enter* R., *go up to Jo, hustle him and get the sovereign.*)

Jo. Now then, what are you doin'? Give me my money, now then.

BUCKET *comes on slowly*, R., *roughs run off*, L., Jo *cries.*

Buc. Now, now, what's all this row about? Come here, you young rascal!

Jo. Oh! ain't I unfortnet.

Buc. Come here.

Jo. Oh! what have I done, Mr. Bucket. Oh! please, Mr. Bucket, don't.

Buc. You know me.

Jo. Yes, Mr. Bucket, because you've moved me on so many times.

Buc. What was all that row about?

Jo. I'll tell you how it was, Mr. Bucket—If you please, sir, I was at my crossin' hard at work, when a lady dressed wery plain in black, and in a weil, came and asked for to be showed the house what him what did the writin' died in, and the buryin' ground where he was buried She says— she says—"Are you the boy what was at the inkwich?" she says; and I says yes—I says. —And she says to me—she says, "Can you show me all them places?" I says "Yes I can" I says;—and she says to me—she says, "Do it"—and I done it, and she give me a sovereign and hooked it, and then them roughs come along and thieved it from me, they did; and then you come along, you did, and asked me what the row was about, and called me a young rascal, you did— That's all, Mr. Bucket, sir.

Buc. Are you telling me the strict truth?

Jo. Yes, Mr. Bucket, I am, sir. I wouldn't tell you a story for the world, sir. [*again?*

Buc. (*Thoughtfully.*) Would you know that lady

Jo. Yes; if she'd got on the weil, and the bonnet, and the gownd.

Buc. Would you? then come along with me.

Jo. He's going to take me to prison. Oh! I'm in for it, again. I am, somehow, unfortnet.

Buc. Come along, sir.

Jo. If you please, Mr. Bucket, sir, let me go, I don't know nothink—I haven't got nothink. Can't you never let such an unfortnet as me alone? ain't I unfortnet enough for you yet? How unfortnet do you want for me to be? I've been chevied and chevied, fust by one and then by another on ye, till I am worrited to skin and bone. The inkwich warnt my fault; I didn't do nothink. He was wery good to me, he was. He was the only one I knowed to speak to as ever come across my crossin'. It ain't wery likely I should want him to be ink- wiched. I only wish I was, myself, and dead, and buried, and then I should never feel cold, nor wet, nor hunger any more. O Mr. Bucket, if you please, sir, if you'll only let me off *this* time, I'll go and make a hole in the water at once, and do away with myself for good.

Buc. Look here, my young shaver, just drop that, and come along quietly.

Jo. (*Blubbering.*) O—O—Oh!—ain't I unfortnet?

Buc. Don't be afraid, I'm not going to take you to prison.

Jo. Where are you goin' to take me?

Buc. You'll see.—I want to bring you and that lady face to face, by and bye, and see if you can identify her.

Jo. But where?

Buc. You'll see—come along! come along!

Jo. Wait a minute, sir, and I'll come—just a minute, sir.

(*Bucket releases Jo, who goes to gate, and takes a long look through it at grave, then carefully brushes the dirt off the steps, and returns to Bucket.*)

A

Jo. (*Tearfully, and in a choking voice.*) He was wery good to me, he was.

[*Exit with Bucket*, L.

SCENE III.—*A Street near Lincoln's Inn.*

Enter GUPPY *with a large bundle of legal documents, meeting* MISS SUMMERSON—*Guppy from* L., *Miss Summerson from* R.

Gup. (*With a start, and dropping the bundle.*) Is it possible? do I behold Miss Hesther Summerson?

Est. That is my name, sir, but——

Gup. 'Tis she, the one I love. You surely recollect me, miss, my name is Guppy, office of Kenge and Carboy, Linkin's Inn. We have met before, when I saw you off in the coach.

Est. Oh! I remember now. How do you do?

Gup. (*Reproachfully.*) How do I do?—Miss, I love you. I have loved you ever since that time. You don't know how I longed to meet you, permiskus like, to plead my soot.

Est. (*Amazed.*) This is quite ridiculous.

Gup. True love always is. (*Esther, going, is detained by Guppy.*) 'Old 'ard miss, (*very mysteriously*) I know secrets that will make you a party to the great Chancery suit of Jarndyce and Jarndyce, and make you rich—yes, rich. It is the dream of my life to serve you.

Est. In what way?

Gup. Time will show. (*Picks up bundle and puts it under his arm; she again trying to escape him, he detains her.*) 'Old 'ard miss—'old 'ard. (*Drops bundle.*) In the mildest language, I adore thee. Say, will you promise to become Mrs. Guppy if I pull this business through, and make you a party to the great soot?

Est. (*Laughing.*) I have no right to be a party to it.

Gup. You have—you shall have—leave it to me. (*She tries again to pass him, but he detains her.*) 'Old 'ard, miss.

Est. You are simply making yourself ridiculous.

Gup. I know I'm not much to look at compared with one like thee, but Miss Summerson, my angel. (*She again tries to pass him, but he detains her.*) 'Old 'ard, 'old 'ard, sweet miss. Ever since the day when I waited for you at the White 'Oss Cellar in Piccadilly, has your himage been bimprinted on my 'art. I have walked up and down, gazin' on the bricks that once contained thee, days and nights have I dreamt of thee; yet now, when I would serve thee, and make thee rich, you spurn me. No matter, I shall still keep on.

Est. You are labouring under a delusion of some kind, and are only making yourself appear ridiculous. Let me pass, and do go and attend to your employer's business.

Gup. (*Detaining her as she is going.*) 'Old 'ard miss. I obey thee, but in case you should think better of what I have said, I give you my private card. (*Takes out a pocket-book, and pulls out with it a short clay pipe, which drops; he picks it up hastily, and puts it away. He gives her a card.*) Address me there. Mr. W. Guppy, 187, Penton Place, Pentonwille; or if removed, or dead, to the care of Mrs. Guppy, 192, Hold Street Road, St. Luke's—near the madhouse. I'll never rest till I've made you a party to Jarndyce v. Jarndyce.

Est. Whatever possesses the man?

Gup. Love miss—love—it's burnin' ere under his weskit like a volcano. Adoo! miss—adoo!—

adoo! We shall meet again. (*Detains her.*) Don't forget—Mr. W. Guppy, 187, Penton Place, Pentonwille; or Mrs. Guppy, 192, Hold Street Road, St. Luke's—near the madhouse.

(*Breaks away from him, and runs off* L. *laughing heartily. Guppy picks up the bundle of papers, and stands for a moment in moody contemplation.*)

Enter CHADBAND, R.

Chad. My dear Mr. Guppy (*Shaking Guppy's hand.*) you are the very one I wanted to see. But why so sad? why so downcast? why is this hand, that I have so often grasped in warmest friendship, so cold and limp?

Gup. Oh! cut it.

Chad. No, I will *not* cut it. How progresseth our little plot? Did you see Lady Dedlock?

Gup. Yes, and she has given me the cold shoulder —cut number one.

Chad. You must persevere, my young friend, you must persevere, and not mind the cold shoulder.

Gup. And now Miss Summerson has given me cut number two. I've been snubbed, sir, snubbed.

Chad. If you will make a love matter of what should be a matter of business, you must expect toe come toe grief.

Gup. Look 'ere, Mr. Chadband, what I'm tryin' to do is all for the benefit of Miss Hesther Summerson. It is for love—not for lucre.

Chad. Love, my young friend, is a snare and a delusion. Not that I have imparted toe you certain facts about Miss Summerson for my own benefit. Oh! dear no. It is only for the love of terewth.

Gup. Oh! cut all that. You're such a humbug. I suppose if anything is made out of it, you'll want to go snacks.

Chad. Yes, my young friend, I *shall* want to go snacks; but only for the love of terewth.

Gup. Now look 'ere—our friend, old Smallweed, Krook's brother-in-law, has got the letters that Krook found, unknown to the coroner, hidden away at the back of a shelf by the side of that fellow Hawdon's bed—ain't he?

Chad. It is so, my young friend.

Gup. Well, you must try and wheedle them out of old Smallweed.

Chad. Well, my young friend, and if I wheedle them out of the venerable Smallweed, what then?

Gup. Why, I shall take them to Lady Dedlock, and if anything good turns up out of it, why, we'll go snacks.

Chad. Verily, you are as seductive as Satan. Well, I will do my best, for the love of terewth.

Gup. Don't—turn it up.

Chad. I will turn it up; but if I get any filthy lucre out of this transaction, I shall devote it toe the spiritual education, and toe the clothing of the naked and benighted heathen, abroad.

Gup. I shall devote mine, what I get, to Miss Summerson.

Chad. Ah! my young friend, woman is an unreliable vessel, a snare and a delusion, toe lure poor, weak man toe his ruin, and toe his destruction. Oh! my young friend, build not your faith on the huming female sect.

Gup. That's all very well for Mr. Snagsby; but *we* know.

Chad. My young friend, do not pervert the terewth.

Gup. I don't—you get the letters, and——

Chad. What, my young friend?

Gup. Look after Mrs. Snagsby.

(*Digs him in the ribs, and hurries off,* R. *Chadband turning up the whites of his eyes with a sanctified air.*)

[*Exit Chadband,* L.

SCENE IV.—MR. TULKINGHORN'S *Chambers.* A good oak set.—*Fire-place and fire,* R.—*table* R. H. *chairs* R. *and* L. *of it—cloth Moderator lamp, alight, and papers on table, with pens and ink. books in bookcase, painted on flat—dark carpet down—wine in bottle, or decanter, on table, and wine glasses—chairs arranged against flats—large key on table—door* L. S. E. HORTENSE *in chair,* L. *of table, dressed in black, and with a black veil over her bonnet; rings on finger.—Her dress to be the same as that worn by Lady Dedlock in scenes* 1 *and* 2 *of this act.* TULKINGHORN R. *of table, warming his hands at fire.*

Hor. (*Impulsively, and gesticulating in French fashion.*) I tell you, Monsieur Tulkinghorn, that I have been shamefully used by my Lady Dedlock.

Tulk. No doubt of it, Mademoiselle Hortense.

Hor. She dismiss me in one moment—and why? because she say I am a spy upon her actions. How should she know, monsieur, that you and I were friends?

Tulk. Why, truly.

Hor. Monsieur Tulkinghorn, I come from the South country, where we are *quick*, and where we like and dislike very strong. My lady is too high for me, I was too high for her. No matter, it is done; I am at your service now. Do wiz me as you like. I do anything for revenge.

Tulk. (*Offering wine.*) A glass of wine.

Hor. Tank you; my most profound respects (*Drinks.*) Oh! it is sweet.

Tulk. What—the wine?

Hor. No—revenge.

Tulk. Ah! you are not very fond of my lady?

Hor. I hate her. I could kill her if it was not for the law, or anyone who did me an injustice.—Why not?

Tulk. Really, mademoiselle, you make me feel quite uncomfortable.

Hor. (*Fawningly.*) I was only joking, monsieur.

Tulk. (*Aside.*) I am not so sure of that.

Hor. What have I to do for you? Come!—quick!

Tulk. Lady Dedlock recently made one of her mysterious and hurried journies to town, on which occasion she wore the very things you now have on.

Hor. Yes, and you me asked to get them, and come here to-night in them. What is that for eh?

Tulk. That is my business.

Hor. I have my suspicions. (*Nodding her head significantly.*)

Tulk. Pray keep them to yourself. Listen now. I am about to leave you for a short time.

Hor. Alone! (*He nods.*)—ah!

Tulk. (*Placing her in position by the side of the table, a little away from the chair on which she has been sitting, and with her face turned towards the door,* L. S. E., *and pulling her veil down.*) I want you to stand thus; and not move until I return.

Hor. (*Alarmed.*) Is not this ver-r-ry str-r-range?

Tulk. Have no fear. When I am gone, that door (*Points to door,* L. S. E.) will be opened, and two persons will enter.

Hor. Am I quite safe? they might murder me.

Tulk. Nonsense!—If you are asked to speak, do so, but hide your foreign accent as much as possible, and merely say: Do you know me?

Hor. Mysteriense! I comprehend.

Tulk. Enough!—Now I must leave you. Remember my instructions. (*Lowers lamp—looks at her—and goes out,* D. L. E.) I shall return.

(*A pause: she stands immovable; presently the door is opened, slowly, and* BUCKET, *leading* JO *by the hand, enters.*)

Jo. (*Catching sight of Hortense.*) There she is.

Buc. Who?

Jo. The lady, I'll swear to her.

Buc. How do you know that to be the lady?

Jo. Why, by the weil, and the bonnet, and the gownd.

Buc. Be quite sure of what you say. Look again.

Jo. I'm a looking as hard as ever I can look, and that there's the weil, and the bonnet and the gownd.

Buc. What about the rings that you told me of.

Jo. (*Rubbing his knuckles.*) What, sparkling all over here? (*Goes quite close to her.*) No—them ain't a bit like 'em; nor the hand ain't a bit like, neither, hers was delicater and whiter.

Buc. Do you recollect the lady's voice?

Jo. Rather!

Buc. (*To Hortense.*) Speak, madam.

Hor. (*Slowly.*) Do—you—know—me?

Jo. That ain't her woice at all.

Buc. Then what did you say it was the lady for?

Jo. (*Perplexed.*) Cos—cos that's the weil, and the bonnet, and the gownd. It's her, and it ain't her. It ain't her hand, nor yet her rings, nor yet her woice. But that there's the weil, the bonnet, and the gownd, and they're wore the same way as she wore 'em, and it's her height what she was, and she give me a sovereign and hooked it.

Buc. That's enough, come with me.

[*Bucket takes Jo off.*

Enter TULKINGHORN.

Tulk. Thank you, mademoiselle, you have played your part admirably, and now, if you please, you may retire; and there (*gives two sovereigns*) is the money I promised you for your trouble.

Hor. Two pounds. Is that all?

Tulk. It is ample, I should think, and very useful to one out of a situation as you are.

Hor. Is it. (*Crosses to* R. *in a passion, and throws the money at his feet up stage.*) There, then; you may want it yourself.

(*Crosses to* L., *nodding her head violently and talking to herself and gesticulating.*)

Tulk. So. You had better pick it up.

Hor. No.

Tulk. Then I will. It is a pity to waste money. (*Picks it up.*)

Hor. Mean! despicable! to pocket money to win a wager as you said, and pay me so poor. You have not used me well, you have been mean—shabby.

Tulk. Mean and shabby, eh?

Hor. (*Goes to* L. *of table, and leans over it, rapping it as she speaks.*) Yes, you have entrapped me to give you information. You have asked me to come here in these things that my lady wore that night, to meet that ragged boy, say, is it not? And you call it a wager. Bah!

Tulk. Well, wench, I paid you. You are a vixen —a vixen.

Hor. You paid me two sovereigns. I have not take them. No, I refuse zem—I despise zem—I throw zem at you. You pick zem up. And you say you have paid me. Ah!—you pay me better, or——

Tulk. What?

Hor. (*Raising her finger menacingly.*) Beware!

Tulk. It is evident to me that you mean to make extortionate demands upon me, and if I don't concede them, you will come here and worry me again and again.

Hor. And again, and yet again, and yet again, and many times again—in effect, for ever.

Tulk. Indeed. Now let me advise you again and again to be wise, to accept these two sovereigns and go.

Hor. I will not.

Tulk. (*Pocketing the money.*) So much the poorer you, so much the richer I. Look mistress, this is the key of my wine cellar. (*Taking up key.*) This is a large key, but the keys of prisons are larger. In this city there are houses of correction, where the treadmills are, the gates of which are very strong and heavy, and no doubt the keys are too. I am afraid a lady of your excitable temperament would find it inconvenient to have one of these keys turned upon you for any length of time. What do you think?

Hor. I think you are a miserable wretch.

Tulk. I don't ask you what you think of *me*; but what of the *prison*?

Hor. Nozing. What does it matter to me?

Tulk. Why, this much, mistress—that the law is so very powerful here that it interferes to prevent a good English citizen being troubled by a lady's visits against his desire, and on his complaining that he is so troubled, the law takes hold of the troublesome lady, and locks her up under prison discipline.

Hor. Truly, this is droll; but what does it matter to me?

Tulk. My fair friend, make another visit here, and you shall learn.

Hor. You would send me to prison—perhaps?

Tulk. Hark ye, if you come here again, I will hand you over to the police. Their gallantry is so great *that* they carry troublesome wenches like you through the streets, strapped fast to a board that they call a stretcher, my good wench.

Hor. I will prove you; I will try if you *dare* do it.

Tulk. Think twice before you come here again.

Hor. And think you twice two hundred times—I go, but—remember!

Tulk. What I say I mean, and what I mean I will do.

Hor. And what I say I mean, and what I mean, I will do—remember! (*Act drop quick.*)

ACT III.

SCENE I.—*Same as Scene IV., Act II.*

TULKINGHORN *and* BUCKET *discovered.*

Buc. That was a long interview with Mademoiselle parlez-vous Francais; I thought you would want the stretcher.

Tulk. Pshaw! a woman's temper, that's all.

Buc. What may be your motive for hunting Lady Dedlock down?

Tulk. The honour of a great and noble family has been tarnished by Sir Leicester's union with her. What has she been? Let her former connexion with that degraded ex-officer and law-writer answer. Is a woman with a dark page in her life fit to be the wife of Sir Leicester Dedlock? Certainly not.

Buc. But look here, sir. They are man and wife, and if you prove her to be the worst woman in the world, what can Sir Leicester do? There's nothing holds so fast as marriage lines, sir.

Tulk. That may be; but she shall be exposed, and her intolerable pride humbled. I have this opinion of Sir Leicester, that if he found she was an unworthy woman, he would no longer live with her.

Buc. Are you ill friends, sir?

Tulk. We hate each other.

Buc. Look here, sir. You applied for a detective officer, and I was told off for the duty. Now I don't mind hunting down a thief, a swindler, or a murderer; but a woman who has once forgotten herself, and has had the good fortune, or the pluck, to get up again, and be respectable, and get a position —damn it! if I like to hunt her down.

Tulk. (*Sneeringly.*) A detective with a conscience!

Buc. Beg pardon, sir—with a heart. Excuse me, sir, you are a very clever old gentleman, no doubt; I say it respectfully, but you may get into trouble if you don't mind. You've got two women to deal with—two women, sir. Now there's a deal of the feline nature in women when they're put out, and between Mademoiselle Hortense and Lady Dedlock you may come to grief; excuse me.

Tulk. What do you mean?

Buc. One of them I know to be a devil, a sly and fierce one when aroused, and you have offended her. She has lost her situation through serving you. Woe to the man who stands between two strong-minded women, and they are both that—the one, burning with hate—the other, maddened with fear of shame and ruin.

Tulk. Mr. Bucket!

Buc. Yes, sir.

Tulk. Will you kindly mind your own business?

Buc. Yes, sir.

(*Takes a glass of wine, re-fills glass and leaves it, so as to be within Chadband's reach later on. A knock at door. Bucket rises and admits* CHADBAND *and* SMALLWEED, *the latter leaning on Chadband's arm. Smallweed is a little weazened old man, of miserly and crabby aspect. He is frequently troubled with a cough that checks his speech.*)

Tulk. (*Recognising Smallweed.*) Well, Smallweed. What do you want? (*To Bucket.*) An old client of mine.

(*Bucket closes door and comes down, quizzing them.*)

Tulk. Just give them a couple of chairs, Bucket.

(*Bucket places two chairs behind them, near table, and himself sits at head of table, leaning his head forward on his hands, watching them, Chadband helps Smallweed to the chair nearest the table.*)

Small. (*As he sits down with difficulty.*) Oh! my bones and back. Oh! my aches and pains.

Buc. What a jolly old guy.

(*Chadband takes the other chair, puts hat and umbrella down beside him, takes off gloves, blows nose, gives a loud ahem! and folds his hands on his knees.*)

Tulk. What is your business, Smallweed?

Chad. (*Rising.*) This gentleman (*points to Smallweed*) is in possession of certain letters, and being animated by the love of terewth——

Small. (*Poking him into the chair with walking-stick.*) Shut up. We don't want a sermon.

Chad. (*Rising.*) I will not shut up. (*Smallweed pushes him again into seat.*) Oh!

(*Hurt, rubs his ribs.*)

Small. I'll tell you what it is :—Snagsby tells me that you want to get at information about that fellow "Nemo." My brother-in-law, Krook, who's dead of internal combustion—and a good job too— found a bundle of letters belonging to him, which I've got in my possession. That fool, Guppy, wants 'em to take to Lady Dedlock; but you shall have them instead, if you'll pay a good price for 'em—that's all. Oh! my bones and back. Oh! my aches and pains.

(*During Smallweed's speech, Chadband slyly reaches behind him, and drains the glass that was filled by Bucket.*)

Buc. All right. Make yourself at home.

(*Chadband, confused, puts the glass in his pocket, and resumes demure attitude.*)

Tulk. Why does Guppy interfere in this affair?

Small. Because he's a brimstone fool.

Tulk. Have you the letters with you?

Small. (*Producing them.*) Yes; here they are. Oh, they are full of secrets—great secrets. Oh! my bones and back. Oh! my aches and pains. You must pay me well for 'em.

Tulk. (*Perusing them.*) I will, if they are worth anything.

Chad. We shall devote the money to the benefit of the naked and benighted heathen abroad.

Small. No, we won't. We'll stick to it.

(*Pours out glass after glass of wine, and drinks; chokes. Chadband pats him on the back.*)

Buc. Serves you right for being greedy.

Tulk. Smallweed, you may trust me with these.

Small. Ain't they good? ain't they capital? Could you oblige me with a little on account?

Tulk. I must see if they are of any value first.

Small. Oh, that's a lawyer all over. Very well, very well. Only, if you don't have 'em, Lady Dedlock will. (*Rises with difficulty by Chadband's help. The latter puts on hat and gloves.*) I'll be going. (*Both move towards door.*) Oh! my bones and back. Oh! my aches and pains.

Buc. (*To Chadband.*) Leave the wine-glass.

(*Chadband takes wine-glass from pocket, and gives it to Bucket, who shows them to the door, and closes it on them, returning to Tulkinghorn.*)

Tulk. (*Rising.*) I would not have missed these for the world. They are in Lady Dedlock's handwriting. (*Looking at letters as he speaks.*) The fervent outpourings of a woman's first affection, and all signed "Honoria," her ladyship's Christian name; and her lover's name was Arthur Hawdon—eh? Now I have her. With these, and what I know besides, I need no more to crush and humble her. She was, then, prior to her marriage with Sir Leicester, connected with that degraded wretch who died at Krook's. These prove it. Shame! shame! Now for Chesney Wold, and my lady. (*Closed in.*)

SCENE II.—*Street near Lincoln's Inn.*

Enter CHADBAND, L., *arm-in-arm with* MRS. SNAGSBY, *followed, at a distance, by* SNAGSBY, *very dejected. Chadband halts about* C.—*Snagsby crosses to* L.

Mrs. S. What is the matter with you, Snagsby?
Snags. Nothing, my love, nothing.
Mrs. S. (*Crossing to Snagsby.*) Don't tell me there's nothing, because I know better. What is this dreadful secret you've got on your poor, small mind?
   (*Business of exchanging glances with Chadband, as if she had touched Snagsby on a vital point.*)
Snags. I've no secrets, my love.
Mrs. S. Don't "love" me! I've told you that twenty thousand million times! Ever since that affair about that wretched scribe who died in a garret you've been melancholy, and about what? (*Hits him in ribs with umbrella.*) You and that old Tulkinghorn are a pair of conspirators. Answer me! (*Bringing her umbrella down on his toes.*) Who was Nimrod?
   (*Winks at Chadband, who nudges her, and points to Snagsby, turning up his eyes.*)
Snags. Nimrod, my dear?
Mrs. S. Yes—Nimrod. (*Spells it.*) N-I-M-R-O-D—rod, which I should like to lay about your back.
   (*Raises umbrella, repeats business with Chadband.*)
Snags. Nimrod—"Nemo," you mean?
Mrs. S. "Nemo," then. Who—was—"Nemo?"
Snags. Well, not to put too fine a point upon it, blessed if I know.
Mrs. S. You can't deceive me, sir. No, sir. Who was Nemo?   (*Repeat business with Chadband.*)
Snags. (*With a whistle of perplexity.*) How should I know?
Mrs. S. And who is that wretched boy? Yes.
   (*Repeat business with Chadband.*)
Snags. What boy?
Mrs. S. You know. You can't blind me. Why, Jo—"Poor Jo," as you call him.
   (*Repeat business with Chadband.*)
Snags. Ah, Jo—poor Jo!
Mrs. S. Poor Jo, indeed. Ever since that inquest you've done nothing but groan out, "Poor Jo!" and "Poor boy!" Oh, you nasty, deceitful little wretch! Where's my winegarette?
   (*Takes out vinaigrette—sniffs at it. Chadband fans her with his hat—She hands bottle to Chadband, who sniffs and sneezes—He takes out pocket-handkerchief from back pocket, and drops cold victuals, which he hastily picks up and re-pockets.*)
Snags. Not to put too fine a point on it, that looks like some of my cold mutton.

Enter JO, *very lame and wretched*, L.

Mrs. S. Ah! there he is. He knows where to find his father.
Jo. (*Looking back at an imaginary policeman as he slowly crosses.*) I'm a-movin' on, sir. I tell you I can't move on no faster. Can't you let a poor boy alone, what never did you any harm?
Mr. S. (*Hitting him with umbrella as he passes her.*) Oh, you ragged little wretch!
Jo. (*Getting quickly to* L. *of Snagsby.*) Mr. Sangsby, sir!
Mrs. S. (*Getting on the other side of Chadband and towards* L. C.) Very well put on, indeed. Well, if he was mine, I'd keep him respectable, anyhow.
Snags. What have you been doing, Jo?
   (*Business as before between Mrs. Snagsby and Chadband.*)

SNAGSBY.   JO.   CHADBAND.   MRS. SNAGSBY.

Jo. Wish I may die if I've done anything. I've never done nothink but what you knows on.
Mrs. S. There.
   (*Looks at Chadband, who turns up his eyes and elevates his hands.*)
Jo. I never was in any trouble, sir, except at that inkwich; but the perlice is allays a chevyin' of me and a movin' me on, and I can't go nowheres but what they does it. I don't know what I've done. I wish I was dead, I do.
Mrs. S. Isn't it well put on?
Chad. Remarkably.
Snags. (*Absorbed in Jo.*) My poor boy!
   (*Burst of indignation from Mrs. S., and more business with scent bottle. Chadband gets nearer to Jo.*)
Jo. I don't want to be a trouble to nobody, I don't. I wish I weren't so unfortnet. (*Looks* L.) There's that perliceman lookin' arter me again. I'm a movin' on, sir—I'm a movin' on!
   (*As he is shuffling off,* R., *Chadband seizes him by the ear and drags him to* C.)
Jo. Oh! let me alone.
Chad. No, my young friend, I will not let you alone. You must receive the lessons of wisdom.
Jo. I don't want 'em; I am hungry and ill.
Chad. But you must bear them, because they will fill your ravenous stomach.
Jo. No, they won't; I've tried 'em afore, and they ain't half so satisfyin' as a basin o' soup.
Mrs. S. (*Hitting him with umbrella.*) You dreadful little heathen!
Jo. (*Writhing in Chadband's grasp.*) Let me go.
Chad. No; you are delivered over toe me, toe your advantage, toe your profit, and toe your enrichment.
Mrs. S. Oh! how delightful.
Jo. I don't want for to be lectured on. Oh! let me go! Oh!
Chad. No, my young friend, I will not let you go. We have here, my friends, a brother and a huming boy.
   Oh! running stream of sparkling joy,
   To be a soaring huming boy.
Snags. I'd set that to the music of a tin kettle.
Mrs. S. (*Hitting Snagsby with umbrella.*) Hold your tongue!
Chad. We have here, my friends, a brother and a huming boy.
Jo. I wish you'd make him turn it up, and le' go o' my hair.
Chad. A huming boy, devoid of friends, devoid of relations, devoid of flocks and herds, devoid of gold, and silver, and copper.
Mrs. S. But not of brass—oh dear no.
Chad. And why of all this? Because he is devoid of the light of terewth.
Jo. I aint. (*Points off* L.) Oh! you'll get me into such a row with that perliceman.
Chad. Peace, brat!—I mean, huming boy. I say it is the ray of rays, the sun of suns, the moon of moons, the star of stars. Say not to me it is not the lamp of lamps. (*Snagsby shakes his head.*) I say it is. I will proclaim it to you whether you

like it or not—nay, the less you like it the more will I proclaim it——

Jo. O—o—oh! my hair!

Mrs. S. (Shaking umbrella at him.) Listen!

Chad. With a speaking trumpet. If you rear yourself against it you shall be floored!—you shall be bruised!—you shall be battered!—you shall be smashed!

(Pulling Jo's head backwards and forwards.)

Jo. You're pullin' all my hair off. If you please, sir, I shall be wery glad to be lectured on some other time. You're wery hard on poor Jo.

Snags. That's the truth.

Chad. (Loudly.) The terewth! I say, what is terewth? If Mr. Snagsby was to go forth from his abode in the City, and there see an eel, and was toe come back, and was toe call untoe him Mrs. Snagsby, and was toe say unto her, "Sarah, rejoice with me, for I have seen an elephant," would that be terewth? (Snagsby holds up his hands in astonishment.) No; or, put it that the parents of this young heathen——

Jo. I never had any.

Chad. (Releasing Jo, and gesticulating with extended arms and his umbrella.) After casting him forth to the wolves, and the vultures—and the wild cats and wild dogs—and the young gazelles—and the brazen serpents—and other wild animals—went back to their dwellings, and had their pipes and their pots—and their flutings and their dancings—and their malt liquors—and their butcher's meat—and their fish, and their poultry—would that be terewth?—(Making a fierce grab at Jo's hair.) No! (Snagsby gives a whistle.)

Jo. (With a shriek.) Oh! he's pulled it all out. Oh! do leave off, sir, you make me feel myself to be so bad and wicked. Ain't I wretched enough without you goin' on at me like this? I know that pleeceman will be down on me directly.

Mrs. S. Do let the little wretch go.

Chad. I will not let him go; for is it right I should have toe wrestle, and toe combat, and toe struggle for his sake.

(Jo is writhing in his grasp all this time.)

Mrs. S. Don't soil your hands any longer with him, dear Mr. Chadband. (Aside.) Let's go home to tea. I've got some nice muffins and watercreeses and shrimps and winkles.

Chad. (Releasing Jo.) Muffins—"watercreeses"—shrimps—and the tasty winkle—I sniff a meal. (Aloud.) I will resoom my discourse on this depraved huming boy some other time.

Mrs. S. (To Snagsby, who hangs back to talk to Jo as she and Chadband go off arm in arm.) Oh! you may stop—we can do without you.

Snags. (Calling softly to Jo.) Jo.

Jo. Oh! let me go, Mr. Sangsby—I shall only get you into a row.

Snags. Jo, my poor boy, come here.

Jo. You had better not talk to me, you'll only get into a row, I tell you.

Snags. I don't care if do. You don't like Mr. Chadband, Jo?

Jo. No.

Snags. Nor his discourses.

Jo. I'd rather run for an hour, than hear him talk for five minutes.

Snags. So would I, Jo. Where have you been since the inquest?—been at Tom All-alone's?

Jo. No; they wouldn't let me go there. I used to sleep there, but I've nowhere to sleep now, except on doorsteps, or under the dark arches; and then they moves me on.

Snags. How is that, Jo?

Jo. I dusn't tell you. I don't know nothink.

Snags. Come, come, Jo!

Jo. No; he'd hear me.

Snags. Who?

Jo. Him what took me to see a lady.

Snags. Who, Jo?

Jo. I dusn't name him—I dusn't, indeed. He'd hear me—Mr. Bucket, I mean—him as was at the inkwich.

Snags. Mr. Bucket. Oh! ah!

Jo. He is a one—er, I can tell you. He's all over the shop, he is; and he's down on me. He is a hot member. He took me to see a lady what I'd shown to the buryin'-ground, and arter that he took me to a horspittle, because I was ill; and arter I was discharged he give me some money—two half-bulls—"And," says he, "now, hook it, because nobody wants you here. You hook it," he says; "you go and tramp," he says; "you move on," he says. "Don't you ever let me see you within forty miles of London, or you'll repent it." So I shall, if ever he does, and I'm above ground. I know he's about here somewhere now.

Snags. Nonsense! What did you do with the five shillings, Jo?

Jo. Went down to Tom All-alone's, and they stole it from me.

Snags. But why does Bucket move you on so?

Jo. Cos he says I blabbed. But don't you ask me. I don't know nothink, and I mustn't.

Snags. I don't know how it is, but everybody who was mixed up with that inquest seems to get into trouble.

Jo. I ain't had no money since Mr. Bucket give me that, and I'm reg'lar hard up, and starvin'.

Snags. They are always giving money to their pet blacks and foreigners abroad. Why the deuce don't they look at home? Poor boy! Why didn't you come to me, Jo?

Jo. Cos I was afeard of Mrs. Sangsby.

Snags. Are you hungry, Jo?

Jo. Oh! ain't I.

Snags. Would a shilling be any good to you, Jo?

Jo. Oh! wouldn't it, sir.

Snags. There, then, Jo. (Gives money.) And what will you do with it, Jo?

Jo. Get some grub.

Snags. And a bed too, at Tom-All-alone's.

Jo. I dusn't get a bed, cos he or some of 'em would come there, and ike me out of it.

Snags. Nonsense! Where will you go, then?

Jo. Right away into the country on tramp, where I ain't known.

Snags. But you'll wear yourself out so.

Jo. I wants to, and then drop down and die. Look, there's that perliceman watching me again. I must move on, I tell you.

Enter POLICEMAN, L.

Jo. I told yer so.

Pol. Now then, move on, d'ye hear? I've been a watching of you.

Snags. Lor' bless you! what harm's he done?

Pol. Don't you hinterfere with the police in the hexecution of their duty.

Snags. It is my duty. What harm's he done?

Pol. He will hang about, and don't move on.

Jo. I'm alays a movin' on, sir. I've allays been a movin' on, an' movin' on, ever since I was born. Where can I possibly move to more than I do move?

Snags. Really, constable, that does seem a question—where?

Pol. I knows where you lives. You lives at Tom

All-alone's; that's a nice innocent place to live in, ain't it?

Jo. They won't let me sleep there now; but if they would I could live in no nicerer place. Who'd go an' let a nice innocent lodgin' to a reg'lar one like me?

Pol. There, you see what a one he is.

Snags. (*Warmly.*) I see what a one you are; such petty tyranny—it's disgraceful! and I've a good mind to write to the papers about it.

Pol. Look 'ere, if the pair of you ain't off sharp I shall take you into custody, and charge you with loiterin' for the purpose of committing a felony—so mind.

Snags. Damn it!—I mean hang it! sir. I'm a respectable man; do you think I would commit a felony?

Pol. I don't think you would, but I should say you would if I took you in charge. You'd better mind—they always believe what a policeman says.

Snags. More shame for 'em. (*Exit Policeman, slowly,* L.) I am afraid they won't let you rest, Jo.

Jo. I told you they wouldn't.

Snags. Jo, here's another shilling for you.

Jo. Oh! sir, you're too good.

Snags. And—and—good-bye—and God bless you, Jo—and—and—there's another sixpence for you, Jo, and if ever you are downright hard up, Jo, and can't get anything, if you come round to my place in the court—Monday and Wednesday evenings are best, Jo, because Mrs Snagsby is out with Mr. Chadband at a mothers' meeting or a tea-fight—and whistle very soft, Jo—like this (*whistles*)—I'll come out and give you a trifle, Jo; and—and not to put too fine a point upon it——Damme! if I can bear to see it! [*Exit abruptly,* R.

Jo. God bless him! Oh! if everybody was only like him. If he'd only got wings he'd be an angel. There's that perliceman watching me again. I must move on. I'm so tired—so tired! Oh!

[*Shuffles off, as policeman slowly crosses.*

SCENE III.—*The Drawing-room at Chesney Wold, as in Act I., Scene IV.*

LADY DEDLOCK and ESTHER *discovered. Lady Dedlock in chair by fireplace, as before. Esther on footstool at her feet.*

Lady D. So, child, you are very happy at Bleak House, with your guardian, Mr. Jarndyce?

Est. Oh! very.

Lady D. He is an excellent-hearted man.

Est. There is not another like him in the whole world.

Lady D. Your early history is shrouded in some mystery, is it not?

Est. (*Sadly.*) It is, indeed.

Lady D. You never knew your parents, I believe?

Est. Never, my lady, I——

Lady D. Poor child. But you were well cared for, were you not?

Est. Oh! yes, my lady. Dear Miss Barbary, my only friend in childhood, watched over and tended me as if I had been her own. Oh! she was so good and kind, although so strict, and stern, and vehement in her denunciation of those who did wrong.

Lady D. (*Pained, a chord of memory touched.*) Let us talk of something else.

Est. Certainly, my lady.

Lady D. Do not call me "my lady;" it is so formal.

Est. Very well, madam.

Lady D. Nor "madam."

Est. (*Timidly.*) What shall I call you?

Lady D. (*Hastily.*) Call me——(*Checking herself.*) Ahem! Do you not wish you had a mother living?

Est. (*Rapturously.*) Oh! how much.

Lady D. What if you know your mother lived?

Est. Ah!—*if* I only knew that.

Lady D. Suppose your mother lived, and you knew her to be the worst woman in the world.

Est. I should pity her, and love her none the less.

Lady D. (*Aside.*) Noble hearted child! Oh! how my heart yearns to break the secret to her. But, no:—I dare not. (*Aloud.*) Have you ever loved?

Est. (*Simply.*) None but my guardian. Have you, my lady?

Lady D. (*Startled.*) I? Why, of course. How should I have wedded Sir Leicester else?

Est. Oh! my lady; but rich folks don't marry for love always.

Lady D. (*Somewhat sadly.*) That is true.

Enter SERVANT, D. L. 2 E.

Ser. My lady, Mr. Tulkinghorn!

Lady D. When did he arrive?

Ser. A few minutes ago, my lady. He wishes to see you on important business.

Lady D. So, he is here again. (*Aloud.*) I will see Mr. Tulkinghorn. (*Servant retires,* D. L. 2 E.) (*Aside.*) I know his business well. (*Aloud.*) Child, leave me, I will see you again.

(*Is allowing Esther to go, when, obeying a sudden impulse of affection, she calls her.*)

Lady D. Come here. (*Esther goes to her.*) Heaven bless you child, and make your life for ever happy.

(*Taking Esther's hands in hers and looking her fondly in the face, and afterwards taking Esther's head in her hands and tenderly kissing her on the forehead. Enter* TULKING-HORN, D. L. 2. E. *He perceives the action, but bows very respectfully; Lady Dedlock, very disdainful, reseats herself, and motions him to a chair. Esther goes off,* R.)

Lady D. Be seated.

Tulk. I thank you. (*Does not sit.*)

Lady D. Be seated, I pray.

Tulk. I thank your ladyship, but I prefer to stand, I have been riding some distance and——

Lady D. On my account, I presume, as Sir Leicester is absent.

Tulk. For the purpose of this interview, my lady. (*With point.*)

Lady D. Ah! (*They regard each other fixedly.*) I am greatly honoured.

Tulk. Your ladyship will—I hope—avoid sarcasm, and rest assured I shall in what I have to say to you. Shall I proceed?

Lady D. (*With an effort to be calm.*) Proceed, sir.

Tulk. 'Tis growing dark. Shall I ring for lights before I begin?

Lady D. No, I like the twilight best. Go on.

(*She is seated—he is leaning over the back of a chair.*)

Tulk. You remember questioning me about the handwriting of the affidavit, and the discovery I made?

Lady D. Perfectly.

Tulk. I am now in possession of most important particulars with reference to the matter.

Lady D. In—indeed.

Tulk. I have discovered that the wretched creature who wrote that affidavit was formerly a captain in the army—a bad dog—a roné. (*Lady D. starts visibly—he perceives it.*) I will not call *names*, nevertheless. There was an episode in his life that affects you.

Lady D. Me?

Tulk. (*Very pointedly.*) Yes, you. Years ago he had become connected with a young girl of respectable family, and—well, my lady—and had ruined her. The birth of a child was the result—a daughter. That child was taken care of by the girl's sister, a woman of strict integrity, who blushed for the shame of her relative; and, when the young mother rose from her sick-bed, she was told that the child was dead, and so it was—dead to her for years, until her stern sister died.

Lady D. What—what has this to do with me?

Tulk. Only this—that the father of the child was named Arthur Hawdon, and the mother of it Honoria Barbary, now Lady Dedlock.

Lady D. What proof have you of all this?

Tulk. These letters, in your handwriting, and signed with your name, which were left by Captain Hawdon at the place where he died.

Lady D. Ah! (*Overpowered by his revelation.*)

Tulk. They contain all these particulars as I have narrated. But I am aware also of your ladyship's visit to Captain Hawdon's obscure grave, which in itself is sufficiently extraordinary to connect your ladyship with him.

Lady D. How long have you known all this?

Tulk. Some days.

Lady D. Have you told any one? Is it the town talk? Is it chalked upon the walls and cried in the streets?

Tulk. Not yet, my lady.

Lady D. Do you know what has become of that child, and whom she is?

Tulk. She is beneath this roof now, and her name is Esther Summerson.

Lady D. What do you intend to do?

Tulk. I do not know what I shall do yet.

Lady D. I neither wish to be spared myself, nor be spared, but spare her. For myself, I leave Chesney Wold this night—this hour. (*He shakes his head.*) What! not go?

Tulk. No, Lady Dedlock.

Lady D. Do you know the relief my disappearance will be? Have you forgotten the stain and blot upon this place, and where it is, and who it is?

(*She rises hurriedly, and crosses to door,* L. 2 E.)

Tulk. (*Moving quietly to bell,* R. *of fireplace, and seizing bell-rope.*) Lady Dedlock, have the goodness to stop and hear me (*She stops*), or, before you reach the staircase, I shall ring the bell, and rouse the house, and then I must speak out before every guest and servant—every man and woman in it.

(*She slowly returns from door, quite crushed and conquered. He points sternly to her former seat, and she resumes it at his bidding.*)

Lady D. (*Humbly.*) Sir, I had better have gone. I have no more to say.

Tulk. (*In former position, leaning over chair.*) Excuse me, Lady Dedlock, and little more to hear.

Lady D. I wish to hear it at the window, there; I can't breathe where I am. (*Music.—Lady Dedlock rises, and slowly goes to the windows,* C., *listening when she reaches windows.*) What is that? Hark! it is the ghost's step. The disgrace has come.

Tulk. Pardon me, not *quite*. At present, the danger only.

Lady D. The danger to Sir Leicester's honour, but to me,—the disgrace *has* come. I can hear the step, and look upon the ghost's face now without fear. Hark! I hear it—tap, tap!

Tulk. It is fancy.

(*Goes up to window, listening, and returns.*)

Lady D. What do you mean to do?

Tulk. Sir Leicester must know all.

Lady D. When?

Tulk. That I cannot say.

Lady D. To-morrow?

Tulk. Perhaps.

Lady D. And then?

Tulk. Then, my lady, what happens will happen.

Lady D. (*Coming down to him,* C.) Spare me.

Tulk. No, Lady Dedlock, no;—emphatically, no! Emphatically, no.

Lady D. May you plead as vainly there. (*Points upward.*) I am prepared. Good night! good night! (*Going towards door,* L. 2 E.) I do not care for myself, but for him who has been so kind to me, and for my poor child. [*Exit,* D. L. 2 E.

Tulk. (*Follows her to door; returns slowly, rubbing his hands, to fire; sits in Lady Dedlock's chair.*) No, no! no mercy, Lady Dedlock, no mercy! Your imposture shall be exposed! Sir Leicester shall be undeceived in the guilty woman he has wedded! He must be; I owe it to him as his faithful servant—friend—and adviser. The family honour is dearer to me than my life. I have much to consider—much. Humph! I must think what is best to be done, and how to break the news to Sir Leicester; but, mercy—I will show her none.

(*Rubs his hands, as he warms them over fire.* HORTENSE, *dressed as in Scene 4, Act 2, and with loaded pistol concealed, glides from behind trees at back, and slowly ascends the steps of the terrace.*)

Tulk. (*Startled and listening.*) Tap, tap! that is the ghost's step surely. I verily believe there is some truth in the legend about the ghost. I believe the ghost is there upon the terrace. Well, I fear no ghosts, whatever others may.

(*Rising and turning.—Hortense has now reached the terrace.*)

Tulk. (*A few steps up stage.*) Good Heaven! the ghost!

Hor. (*With the French accent.*) No—no ghost, but a woman who has sworn revenge!

(*She fires, and he falls. The lime light is thrown full upon her, as she stands pointing at Tulkinghorn.*)

END OF ACT III.

ACT IV.

SCENE 1.—*Another apartment at Chesney Wold. Folding Doors,* C.—*Lights up.*

LADY DEDLOCK *enters.*

Lady D. Who could have done this foul murder? Oh! I would to Heaven it had not been done! With my provocation, I might be suspected of it, if all were known! Is it known? I have looked upon his face, and it seemed as if Death had set his dread seal upon my secret. But what of that, since I accuse myself?

Enter FOOTMAN, *who gives her a letter, and retires.*

Lady D. (*As she breaks the seal.*) Who could have

done this murder? (*Reads letter.*) "Lady Dedlock, murderess!"
(*Music chord.—She utters a loud cry, and falls on the chair. The face of Hortense is seen at back. She points with gratified malice to Lady D., and retires.*)

Lady D. (*Bewildered.*) "Lady Dedlock, murderess!" Oh, horror! horror!

Enter ESTHER, L., *who goes to her.*

Est. Madam. (*To* R. *of Lady D., trying to rouse her.*) Madam.
Lady D. Yes. What—what is it?
Est. You wrote to me to come. You said you had a secret to reveal.
Lady D. Oh! my child! my child! I am your guilty and unhappy mother!
(*Music.—Drops on her knees in front of chair, burying her face in her hands.*)
Est. Oh! my mother! rise and let me kneel and thank you for this confession!
(*Trying to raise her, but vainly.*)
Lady D. Oh! my heart has thirsted so for your love! I am so wicked—so guilty!
(*Buries her face in Esther's lap, as Esther drops.*)
Est. Guilty!—you?
Lady D. Yes, I. (*Looking up.*)
Est. No guilt of yours, dearest mother, could change my love for you. Though the whole world should turn from you, I still would cling to you—thus, heart to heart, and thus, with love, bless and receive you! (*Pressing Lady D. to her.*)
Lady D. Bless and receive me! It is far too late. I must travel my dark road alone. From day to day, from hour to hour, I do not see the way before my guilty feet. This is the earthly punishment I have brought upon myself. I bear it, and I hide it.
Est. Hide it—hide what? (*Lady D. covers her face.*) Rise—rise.
Lady D. No, no, no! I can only speak to you thus. Everywhere else I should be proud and disdainful, but here, in the only natural moments of my life, I will be humbled and ashamed. (*Takes letter from bosom, gives it to Esther.*) Read that, it is my sinful history.
Est. No, no!
Lady D. (*Forcing letter on her.*) Read it—read!
Est. (*Unwillingly glancing at it.*) What? "Henceforth consider me as dead, now that you know my secret."
Lady D. It must be so. Read, I say! (*While Esther peruses letter, Lady D. watches her closely, and as she looks up from the letter, turns her head as if ashamed.*) What are your thoughts?
Est. (*Raising and embracing her.*) To love you more and more.
Lady D. Why do you not shrink from me?
Est. What I, your child?
Lady D. Oh! do, do. Shun me, hate me. 'Twill make our parting less bitter.
Est. Our parting?
Lady D. (*Looking at letter given by Footman.*) I must leave this place.
Est. Whither to go?
Lady D. (L. *of Esther, and with icy emphasis.*) Through the desert that lies before me. I must go alone.
Est. I will go with you.

Lady D. (*To herself.*) Alone! alone! alone!
(*She gradually breaks from this mood, and suddenly embraces Esther with passionate warmth.*)
Lady D. O my child, my child, for the last time these kisses—these arms upon my neck for the last time. To hope to do what I seek to do, I must no longer be what I have been so long. Such is my reward and my doom. If ever you think of your mother, think of her suffering, of her useless remorse, in murdering within her breast the only love and truth of which she is capable, and then forgive her, if you can, and cry to Heaven to forgive her, which it never can. Farewell! We shall never meet again.
(*She kisses Esther passionately, and hurries off* R. *followed by her.*)

Enter SIR LEICESTER *and* BUCKET, D. C.

Sir L. (R. *of Bucket*). And is it possible, sir, that she whom I have so loved and trusted, could have had so dark a page in her life?
Buc. I'm sorry to say it is, Sir Leicester Dedlock, Baronet, and here are these letters that I spoke of to prove it. Read for yourself. (*Offers letters*).
Sir L. No, sir; I will not read the history of her shame. More shame to those who have broken the privacy of her correspondence to make her disgrace more apparent to one who would rather he had died than known it.
Buc. (*Aside.*) Damme! if that isn't noble! Sir Leicester Dedlock, Baronet, will you allow me, Inspector Bucket, of the Detective, to shake hands with you? (*Sir Leicester gives hand.*)
Sir L. Mr. Tulkinghorn was my solicitor—nay, more, he was my friend; but, had I known that he was labouring to undermine and blast my lady's noble character, had he been twenty times the friend he was—nay, more, had he been my own brother, I would never have spoken to, or acknowledged him again. Why, sir, have you told me this?
Buc. Because, Sir Leicester Dedlock, Baronet, you may as well know what others know. Because there is a cunning she-devil at work who knows some of these facts, and would make Lady Dedlock out to be——
Sir L. Great Heaven! what?
Buc. A murderess! (*Chord*).
Sir L. (*Catching at chair,* R, *and sinking into it*). Great Heaven!
(*A great noise outside of voices.*)
Buc. Hullo! what the deuce is all that?
(*Goes to door, throws it open, and discovers Chadband, Smallweed, and Mrs. Snagsby arguing with servant.*)
Buc. (*Easily.*) Oh! it's you, is it? Come in! Come in!

They enter. CHADBAND R. *of* MRS. SNAGSBY. SMALLWEED L. *of them.*

(*Bucket recloses door and dismisses servant, and comes down* L. *of Smallweed. All to front.*)
Glad to see you. What do you want, eh?
Small. You know. You brimstone cheat, you!
(*Shaking his fist at Bucket.*)
Buc. (*To Smallweed, taking out small staff from his breast pocket.*) I'm Inspector Bucket, of the Detective, and this is my authority; and you be respectful to it, or I'll let you know the reason why you should be. You're name is Smallweed, isn't it?

Small. Yes, and you never heard any harm of it.

Buc. I never heard any good of it. You don't happen to know why they killed the pig, do you?

Small. No.

Buc. Well, they killed him because he'd too much cheek. Now just be good enough to pitch your voice an octave or two lower, will you? The other gent is in the preaching line, isn't he?

Small. Yes.

Buc. Of course; we've met before. Now what have you all come here for?

Small. Why, about those letters.

Buc. Well, what about 'em.

Small. I haven't been paid for 'em. I've been cheated out of 'em, and I want to know where they are. I handed 'em over to my friend and legal adviser, Mr. Tulkinghorn, and he's dead, and I'll know who's got 'em.

Buc. I have—and what's more, mean to keep 'em.

Small. You—you—you—(*Falls into a violent fit of coughing.*) (*To Chadband.*)—You speak for me.

Buc. Ah! let's hear what you've got to say, only cut it short.

(*He takes a chair and places it so that he sits astride of it, with his hand on the rail.*)

Chad. (*Taking out his handkerchief and mopping his face.*) My friends, why are we now in the mansions of the rich and great? Is it because we are invited—because we are bidden to feast with them? (*Bucket nods his head as Chadband speaks.*)—because we are bidden to play upon the lute with them? No. Then why are we here my friends? *Air* we in possession of a sinful secret, and *does* we require corn and oil, or what is much the same thing—money—for the keeping thereof? Probably so, my friend.

Buc. Then you won't get it, so you may as well hook it at once. Have you got anything to say, ma'am?

(*To Mrs. Snagsby.*)

Mrs. S. Yes, a good deal. I'm a deeply injured woman; but I don't want to lower myself by speaking to a common policeman.

Buc. That's right—don't. (*Rises and pushes chair away.*) Look 'ere—there's enough misery in this house without you coming here to make matters worse. What do you two want to keep you quiet?

(*To Smallweed and Chadband.*)

Small. I want to be paid for those letters.

Buc. And suppose you don't get paid, what then?

Chad. Then, my friend, in the interests of terewth, we shall have to make the matter of the letters public.

Buc. And what do you ask for keeping matters to yourself, my friend?

Small. Five hundred pound.

Buc. Make it a thousand while you're about it. Now, look here, shall I settle this matter at once?

Small. You'd better, you brimstone cheat! or——

Chad. Peace, my friend.

Small. Peace yourself, you preaching magpie!

Buc. Suppose I say I shan't give you anything, what then; what would the letters prove?

Small. Why, you brimstone idiot, wouldn't they prove who Lady Dedlock was, and the motive that she had for putting Mr. Tulkinghorn out of the way?

Chad. It is so, my friend.

Buc. (*Putting his hands in his pockets, and coolly surveying them.*) You'd hang a woman on suspicion, would you? Upon my word you're a nice pair, what ought to be whipped at the cart's tail. Now, I'll tell you what, I'm hanged if I'm going to have my case spoilt, or interfered with, or anticipated by half so much as a second of time by anybody. Do you see this hand, and think that I don't know the right time to stretch it out and put it on the arm that fired that shot. (*Very hotly. Goes up and throws doors open, and comes down.*) Now, look here! just you be off, the lot of you, or I'll deuced soon have you pitched out head foremost.

Mrs S. What, pitch me out?

Buc. No, ma'am, I'm not so ungallant as to do that, but I shall *hand you out* with all the respect in the world. (*Hands out Mrs. S.*, D. C. *Returns to Smallweed.*) And now *you* be off, or I'll take you into custody for conspiracy.

Small. You, you—— (*Shaking with passion.*)

Buc. If you please, be off! (*Bonnets him as Smallweed gets out at door*, C. *Returns to Chadband.*) Now, Mr. Mawworm, be off.

Chad. Don't touch me. I see you are a sinful man of war.

Buc. Yes, and I'll deuced soon put a broadside into you if you don't hook it. (*Comic business with Chadband as the latter tries to get out. Gets a kick at Chadband as the latter gets out*, D. C. *Returns to Sir L.*) Now, you see, Sir Leicester Dedlock, that there are a good many more people ready and willing to fix this shame on Lady Dedlock. But never mind them. Now, with regard to the party to be apprehended——

Sir L. (*Rising, and with profound emotion.*) Have a care, sir! have a care.

Buc. The party to be apprehended is at present in this house.

Sir L. You would not—you dare not mention my lady's name in connection with such a foul crime!

Buc. No; but it is mentioned, and pretty freely too. Look here! (*Shows letter.*) There has been latterly a heap of these letters flying about—addressed to everybody. Here's one to me, addressed Mr. Inspector Bucket, right enough; but what's inside? It says—"Lady Dedlock, murderess!"

Sir L. (*Sinking into chair, overpowered.*) This is terrible!

Buc. It is a disguised hand, you see. Now with respect to the party to be apprehended, as I said before, that party is at present in this house.

(*Sir Leicester is quite speechless with excitement.*)

Buc. And I'm about to take her into custody in your presence.

(*Sir Leicester rises, nervously protesting.*)

Buc. Now, don't be nervous. Sir Leicester Dedlock, Baronet, you shall see the whole case clear from first to last.

(*Goes to door, whispers to Footman, and stands behind door with his arms folded.*)

Enter HORTENSE, D. C.

(*Bucket claps the door to, and puts his back against it.*)

Hor. (C. *Startled, to Sir Leicester.*) I ask your pardon. They tell me there was no one here.

Buc. This is my lodger, Sir Leicester Dedlock. She has been my lodger for some weeks back.

Hor. What do Sir Leicester care for that, you think, my angel?

Buc. Why, my angel, we shall see.
(L. *of Hortense.*)
Hor. You are very mysterious. Are you drunk?
Buc. Tolerably sober, my angel.
Hor. I come from arriving at this detestable house with your wife. She has left me since some minutes. They tell me down-stairs that your wife is here; and she is not here. What is the intention of this fool's play? Say then.
(*Bucket shakes his finger at her.*)
Hor. Ah, *mon Dieu!* You are an unhappy idiot. (*Makes a movement to go up to* C. *doors.*) Bucket, leave me to pass down-stairs, great pig!
Buc. Now, Mademoiselle Parley-vous-Francais, you go and sit down upon that sofy.
(*Catches her by a quick movement with his right hand by her left wrist, and pointing to sofa.*)
Hor. I will not sit down upon nothing.
(*Nodding violently.*)
Buc. (*Pointing still to sofa.*) Now, mademoiselle, you sit down upon that sofy.
Hor. Why?
Buc. Because I take you into custody upon a charge of murder, and you don't need to be told of it. Now, I want to be polite to one of your sex, and a foreigner, if I can. If I can't, I must be rough; and there's rougher ones outside. What I am to be depends on you. So I recommend you, as a friend, afore another half a blessed moment has passed over your head to go and sit down upon that sofy.
(*She complies, but reluctantly.*)
Hor. You Bucket, you are one devil!
Buc. Now, look here; be a lady, and the less you parley the better.
Hor. Oh!—you Bucket, you are a devil!
Buc. Now, Sir Leicester Dedlock, Baronet, this young woman was, as you know, her ladyship's maid, and this young woman, being extraordinarily vehement and passionate against her ladyship after being discharged——
Hor. Lie! I dischar-rge myself!
Buc. Now, mind. What you say will be given in evidence. Take my advice, and don't parley.
Hor. Dischar-rge, too, by her ladyship! Eh! my faith! a pretty ladyship! Why, I r-ruin my character by remaining with a ladyship so infame.
Buc. Upon my soul, I wonder at you. I thought the French were a polite nation. Yet to hear a female going on like that before Sir Leicester Dedlock, Baronet.
Hor. He is a poor abused—I spit upon his house —upon his name! Oh!—that he is, a great man! Oh! yes; superb! Heaven! Bah!
Buc. You will parley, you know. This young woman took it in her head that she had a claim upon the late Mr. Talkinghorn, by attending on the occasion I told you of at his chambers. I believe she was paid for her time and trouble.
Hor. Lies! I refuse his money altogezzer.
Buc. If you will parley, you know—— Now observe: this young woman, after she left her ladyship's service, became my wife's lodger. As she was sitting at supper, one night, by Heaven! it flashed upon me, as I sat opposite to her at the table, and saw a knife in her hand, that she had done it.
Hor. You are a devil! (*Goes suddenly to door.*)
Buc. (*Bringing her back.*) Now, don't you do that again, or I shall link your feet together at the ankles. I'll sit down by you, my angel. I'm a married man, you know. You're acquainted with my wife, and she isn't jealous; just take my arm. (*Sits to* L. *of her, and takes her arm.*) Now, what has she tried to do? Why, throw the suspicion on her ladyship.
Hor. All lies.
Buc. She has been writing heaps of letters, with "Lady Dedlock, murderess," in every one. Now, my wife has seen her write them—every one, and post them, and secured the corresponding ink, and sheets, and what not.
Hor. (*Faintly.*) Lies!
Buc. And a piece of printed paper that corresponds with the wadding of the pistol. That looks like Queer Street; don't it?
Hor. These are very long lies. You prose a great deal. Is it that you have almost finished?
Buc. Nearly. One day she went to some tea-gardens with my wife, near which there's a piece of water, into which she was seen to throw a parcel, which was dragged up by our men afterwards, and found to contain a pistol.
Hor. Oh!—you devil!
Buc. Now for the last bit of evidence. In her box my wife found a dress like that worn by the Ghost, an unusual thing for a young lady to wear. Now, ghosts have been humbugs before to-day; and perhaps the Dedlock ghost was all humbug. I don't say it was; but, after mademoiselle left, the Ghost was never seen on the terrace. But on the night of the murder the Ghost *was* seen upon the terrace, as I can prove, and the window was wide open. It strikes me, mademoiselle, you had played the Ghost at Chesney Wold, and on *that* night. Now, my dear, put your arm a little through mine, and hold it steady, and I sha'n't hurt you. (*Slips on handcuffs.*) That's one; now the other. Two, and all told.
Hor. Oh! I would like to kiss your wife!
Buc. You'd bite her, I expect.
Hor. I would. I would tear her limb from limb.
Buc. You don't mind me?
Hor. No, though you are a devil still. Let me put your shawl tidy. (*Arranges shawl.*) I've been lady's maid to a good many before. Anything wanting to the bonnet? Come along.
Hor. Can you make an honourable lady of her or a haughty gentleman of him, eh? Oh! then, regard him, the poor infant! Ha! ha! ha! Adieu! you old man gray. I pity and I des-pise you!
[*Taken out by Bucket.*
Buc. Come, this is worse parleying than the other.

(*Sir Leicester sits in a stupor, quite broken down now.*)

Sir L. And can she whom I have so loved and admired, and set up for the world to respect, have been all that he has said she was? No, no; I will *not* believe it. I cannot bear to see her cast down from the high place she has graced so well.

Enter BUCKET *hastily, with* ESTHER SUMMERSON.

Buc. Sir Leicester Dedlock, Baronet, her ladyship has sent this letter to you by Miss Summerson.
Sir L. (*Breaks seal and reads.*) What's this? (*Reads.*) (*Music, tremo.*) "If I am sought for or accused of murder, believe that I am wholly innocent. Believe no other good of me, for I am guilty." Guilty! "I have no home left; I will

encumber you no more." Oh! "I will only ask you to watch over my unhappy daughter, who brings you this, and think of her sometimes, though she is not uncared for. May you, in your just resentment, be able to forget the unworthy woman on whom you have wasted a most generous devotion—who avoids you with only a deeper shame than that with which she hurries from herself, and who writes this last adieu."

(*He drops the letter, then with a loud cry sinks into the chair. Rising, recovering after a moment or two.*)

Sir L. Is—is she dead.

Buc. No—but she has left the house.

Sir L. Officer, pur—pursue her—bring her back—tell her I bless and pardon her. Take Miss Summerson. Spare no expense. I'd give my fortune—my life—to rest my eyes on her once more.—Pur—pur—sue—bring her back.

(*Falls in chair as scene is closed in.*)

SCENE II.—*In the vicinity of Chesney Wold,*—(1st *Grooves.*—*Lights up.*)

Enter GUPPY *and* SNAGSBY, L. (*Guppy first.*)

Gup. Rejected—scorned—refused—despised—snubbed—Ha! ha!

Snags. My dear Mr. Guppy, what is the matter?

Gup. The matter. Have I not interested myself on behalf of one whom I madly adore—I mean adored. Have I not dived into matters that did not concern me for the purpose of making the one I love —I mean loved—a party to Jarndyce and Jarndyce.

Snags. You have.

Gup. And what is my reward? There is a letter in which I am told to mind my own business, and that nothing I can say, or do, or find out can be of the slightest interest to her.

Snags. Then we have come all this way for nothing!

Gup. My dear Snagsby, we have expended the price of two third-class return tickets for nothing, which, however, I stand. Understand me, as a friend—the idol is down—the image is smashed. I have no purpose to serve now but burial in oblivion. To that I have pledged myself in the last interview I shall ever have with her. If you was to express to me by a gesture or a wink that you saw lying anywhere, any papers that so much as looked like the letters about which I have so deeply interested myself, I would pitch you into the fire, sir, on my own responsibility.

Snags. Really—upon my word, trouble and annoyance seems to come to everybody that is mixed up with this business—Mr. Tulkinghorn has come to an untimely end, and you are in a fair way to do so too—and there's that poor lad, Jo, too —and as for me (*with a sigh*), where peace once reigned in my little abode of bliss in Cook's Court there is now discord and the jangling of tongues. My little woman gives me no rest day or night.

Gup. Snagsby, it would be folly to conceal from you that between myself and the members of a swan-like aristocracy there has been undivulged communication and association. The time might have been when I might have revealed it to you. It never will be more—as I before observed—the idol is smashed, and my dream is o'er. Snagsby, I'm a blighted being.

Enter SMALLWEED, CHADBAND, *and* MRS. SNAGSBY, L.

Snags. What! my little woman!

Chad. Ah! my dear Mr. Snagsby, how are you?

Snags. Well, sir, as well as can be, under the circumstances.

Mrs S. Under what circumstances? What do you mean to insinuate?

Snags. Nothing, my love, nothing; only I thought you were at home, looking after the shop.

Mrs. S. Looking after the shop, indeed; while you are galavanting about, Lord knows where, with that fool from Kenge and Carboy's.

Gup. Madam,—I beg your pardon; but go it. I am down now—Let me have it—Please to let me have it hot all round. Rejected—scorned—refused —despised—snubbed—ha!

Chad. My friend, we have all been snubbed.

Gup. Get out, you oily humbug!

Chad. Be calm, my friend.

Small. What is the matter with that brimstone fool? (*Coughs.*) Oh! my bones and back, oh! my aches and pains.

Gup. I'll knock you into the middle of next week, if you talk to me, you old scarecrow!

Small. (*Snarling.*) Yah! you dog! you brimstone barker! yah! (*Coughing violently, and shaking stick at him.*)

Chad. Peace, my friends, peace. (*To Guppy.*) My friend, if you have been ensnared, and entangled, have we not also? Have we not trusted in our Tulkinghorns and our Buckets, and been deceived? Have we not been toilers and moilers to no purpose?

Gup. If you'd stuck to me all would have been right; but no, you wouldn't, you must go and take the letters to old Tulkinghorn, to make money of 'em.

Chad. My friend, is this *terewth*?

Gup. Blow *terewth*, you've got no *terewth* about you. You are a mean, deceitful, slimy, oily sneak! —and as for that old guy——

Small. Touch me, if you dare! Oh! if somebody would only get me a paving stone, to throw at him.

Chad. My friends, peace. Let me pour oil upon the troubled waters. (*Rubs his hands.*)

Small. Pour brimstone—brimstone!

Gup. Look 'ere, you took the letters, you and that old Smallweed there, to Tulkinghorn. I wanted 'em for a good purpose; I didn't want to harm anybody; but you didn't care what happened to anybody so long as you made money. Old Tulkinghorn's dead, and we've got nothing for *those precious letters.*

Small. We've been outwitted—done! Oh! brimstone furies! I should like to burn and smash everybody—I should!

Gup. So should I—And smash everybody I will, if they don't get out of the way. Snagsby, come on, stick tight to me, don't let me go, or I shall certainly do myself a violence. Rejected—scorned —refused—despised—snubbed. Ha! ha! ha!

[*Rushes out,* R., *followed by Snagsby. Chadband, Mrs. Snagsby, and Smallweed follow*

Small. (*Coughing as he goes off.*) Oh! my bones and back! oh! my aches and pains!

SCENE III.—*A Wild and Bleak Track of Country.* —*Lights quite down*—*Storm Music*—*Storm and Crash.*

LADY DEDLOCK, *meanly dressed, weather-beaten and wretched, enters at back,* R.

Lady D. (*Shrinking from the storm, and moving as if over rough and uneven country.*) Oh! what a dreadful night! I think that I shall die with terror, or go mad! I dare not turn back! No, no; I must go onward! (*Crash and flash*, L, *drives her back as she is going*, L.) Oh! this is dreadful! (*Gets back.—Rain.*) I am drenched to the skin! What shall I do? where go? I see no shelter! I must go onward, onward, but where? (*Crash and flash.*) Merciful Heaven! Oh! am I not punished? I am chilled to the bone! Where shall I rest till the storm is over? (*A noise off* L, *as of wheels.*) What's that? (*Shouts off "Hi! hi!"—She listens and looks* L.) A carriage is coming this way! (*Shouts off* L, *as of urging horses on.*) They are after me! I must fly! (*Going* R.—*Crash and flash* R. *repeated, which drives her back. She sinks down* C.) They must come! I can endure no more!

(*By a great effort rises and rushes off* R, *as* BUCKET, *carrying a lantern, enters with* ESTHER L.)

Buc. What a nuisance the carriage breaking down. But never mind, I've sent the postillion forward on one of the horses to the next village, to see if he can get a wheelwright.

Est. Promise me you'll not abandon the pursuit.

Buc. Oh no, miss; not I. It's awkward. Just as we were on the right scent, too. I know she changed clothes at the cottage where she left this paper.

Est. What does it say?

Buc. No, miss; no.

Est. Do—do read it. I can bear the worst.

Buc. I know you've got pluck, my dear. Well, I'll read it if I can. (*Reads paper by light of lantern.*) "I have wandered a long distance, and for many hours, and I know that I must soon die. Cold, wet, and fatigue are sufficient causes for my being found dead; but I shall die of others, though I suffer from these. It was right that all that had sustained me should give way at once, and that I should die of terror and my conscience. I have done all I could to be lost. Farewell! Forget—forgive! (*He puts back paper.*) Cheer up, my dear!

(*A cry off* R. *by Lady D. He listens.*)

Buc. That is a woman's cry, I'll swear. Hark! (*Cry repeated.*) Come with me.

[*Goes off with Esther* U. E. R. *Crash and flash* R. *as they go off.*

LADY DEDLOCK *staggers on*, R.

Lady D. My strength and courage fail me. I can go no further. Yet, if Heaven had but given me strength to reach his lonely grave.

Enter BUCKET *and* ESTHER, U. E. R.

Buc. I'll swear she came this way.

(*Perceives Lady D. Goes to her. Holds lantern near her face. Recognises her.*)

Est. Oh! what is the matter? Speak!

Buc. (*Reverently*). Your hands should be the first to touch her.

(*Esther kneels over Lady D. Recognises her.*)

Est. My mother! (*Kissing her, as she raises her head.*) Speak to me! speak to me! Ah! she is cold and dead!—cold and dead!

SCENE IV.—*Exterior of Snagsby's.—Lights quarter down.—Jo's music. A practicable step to let down in front of Snagsby's door.*

Enter JO, L.

Jo. Oh! I'm so weak and ill! I'm starved and dying; I am, I know I am; and I ain't got a friend in the world, except—except it's Mr. Snagsby. I wish I could see him. He told me if I was hard up to come to him, and if I whistled very soft he'd come out if Mrs. Snagsby wasn't in. I—I—I'll try and whistle—if—if—I can. (*Tries to whistle, but can't.*) I can't—I—I ain't got breath enough. (*Coughs.*) I wish he'd come out.

(*Tries again, and whistles, but very faintly, and with great effort, and coughs. He cautiously stands aside, watching the door in fear of Mrs. Snagsby. The door is opened slowly, and Snagsby comes out.*)

Snags. Jo!—Jo!

Jo. Is that you, Mr. Snagsby?

Snags. Yes, Jo. (*Closes door gently, and goes to Jo.*) How are you, Jo?

Jo. Oh, bad, sir; wery bad.

Snags. I'm sorry for that, Jo. Are you hungry, Jo? (*Producing some bread and meat from his pocket, and some beer in a bottle.*) Come and sit down, and eat and drink something.

(*Jo is very nervous, and hesitates, looking towards house.*)

Snags. You needn't be afraid, Jo. My little woman is out with her spiritual adviser. They've gone to a tea-fight—(*whistles*)—where there's to be a collection afterwards for the poor blacks that cannot read and write, and are not blessed with the light of terewth. I keep my money for the poor little black faces at home that are more in need of it. Come now, Jo, eat, drink, and—be merry.

(*Jo tries a morsel or two, seated on step, but cannot eat. Puts food down.*)

Jo. I—I can't, sir.

Snags. Try a little beer, Jo, poor fellow. It will do you good.

(*Jo drinks a little, and puts bottle down.*)

Jo. I can't; it burns me like.—(*Puts hands to throat.*) Oh! my throat does burn so.

Snags. Well, not to put too fine a point upon it. This makes me very miserable. Jo, do try.

(*Offers bottle.*)

Jo. No, no, sir; thankee.

Snags. Jo, whatever's the matter?

Jo. I'm bein' froze, I am, to death, and then burnt up, and then froze again, and then burnt up ever so many times; and my head's all sleepy, and a goin' mad like, and I'm so dry, and my bones ain't half so much bones as pain.

Snags. It's a fever.

Jo. That's it, and it's why they moves me on. Oh! they have moved me on. "You ain't a goin' to stop here and breed fevers," says one. "You're poisonin' our place," says another. "You're a hidle rogue, and a wagabone," says another. When I goes to the workhouse, they says—they says, "We're full; go somewhere else." Yes, the workhouse chucks me out; and the bobbies won't run me in—they only moves me on. And so I wanders about like a dog—like a dog.

Snags. O, Jo, Jo; if it wasn't for my little woman, I'd take you in, and do something for you.

Jo. Would you, sir? God bless you! God bless you! (*Coughs.*)

Snags. Now if I had that cough I cou'd bear it, because I'm a strong, hearty, healthy man.

(*Slaps chest, the blow makes him cough violently.*)

Jo. Oh! I feel so ill. I say, Mr. Sangsby, I tell yer where I wants for to be taken in. (*Points to house.*) Not there; cos she'd chevy me.

Snags. I—I'll be hanged if she should.

Jo. I'll tell you, sir, where I wants to be taken.

Snags. Where, Jo?

Jo. To the buryin' ground, sir; where he is as was so wery good to me.

Snags. Why—why so?

Jo. Cos there, sir, I should be at peace. Do take me there, sir; will you? I—I want to go there. (*Rises, very faint.*) But I won't trouble you, Mr. Sangsby, I can go by myself. I—I don't want for to get you into no—no rows. Besides, I've got the fever. I—I can go alone. (*Music.*) God—God bless you, Mr. Sangsby! Hush! No, no! (*Points warningly with finger, and crawls off, R., staggering with weakness.*) Don't come! don't come!

Snags. (*Stands a moment irresolute; then bursts out.*) I will come, if my little woman hangs me for it.

[*Rushes after Jo, R.*

SCENE V.—*The Churchyard.*—*Lights down to suit double lime-light, which is on from beginning to end of scene.*—*Jo's music.*

Enter SNAGSBY *and* JO, R.

Snags. Jo, my poor fellow, how do you find yourself?

Jo. Worse, sir—worse, and more fainter. I'm thankful, though, you're with me, cos—cos I wants to make my will afore I die.

Snags. Jo, my poor lad!

Jo. I'm in luck, I am, Mr. Sangsby, and I don't want for nothink now I'm here. I'm more comf'-bler now than ever I was afore.

(*Several poorly-dressed people enter, R. and L., and stop as if arrested by the sight of Jo so ill and weak. They group round. Jo, C., supported by Snagsby.*)

Jo. All the pain's gone away, and I feel happy like. (*A pause*). What I was a-thinkin' of was, Mr. Sangsby, that when I was moved on as fur as ever I could go, and couldn't be moved no furder, whether you might be so good as to write out very large, perhaps, so that any one could see it unawares, that I was wery truly sorry for the trouble I've been to everybody in the world, and that I hope the Lord will forgive me. If the writin' could be made wery large, I'd be thankful.

Snags. It shall—it shall.

Jo. Thank you, Mr. Sangsby; it's wery kind on yer.

Enter BUCKET, L.

Buc. (*Softly*). What's on here? (*Goes C.*) What, Jo!

Jo. O, Mr. Bucket, don't—don't move me on, sir! I'm a-movin' as fast as I can. (*Tries to rise*).

Buc. My poor lad, don't be afraid!

Jo. Don't chevy me.

Buc. No, no; they sha'n't chevy you any more. (*Music.—Other people enter and group.*)

Jo. I should have died long ago, if they'd let me alone, but they wouldn't give me time to die. I used often to lie down to sleep and wished I might not wake again, but they allays woke me up, and moved me on.

Snags. But that's all over now.

Jo. I know it is. It was my fault, I s'pose, for bein' so wery unfortnet—but it don't matter now. (*Coughs.*) My breath's very hard to—to draw. I think I'm dyin'.

Snags. Jo, my poor lad, do you know a prayer?

Jo. No, sir, none at all. I never knowed nothink.

Snags. Have you never heard of Heaven, Jo?

Jo. Heaven!—heaven! (*A pause.*)

Snags. Heaven, Jo. There. (*Pointing upward.*)

Jo. I—I have heerd o' that. That's where they lets poor lads like me in.

(*Jo half-rises to his feet, but does not move from the spot; he is supported by Snagsby and Bucket.*)

Jo. I say, Mr. Sangsby and Mr. Bucket, it's time for me to get to that berryin'-ground where he is what was so wery good to me. (*They help him to his feet.*) It's time for me to be put along with him. I wants for to be buried there. He used for to say, "I'm as poor as you, Jo, to-day," and I wants to say that I'm as poor as him now, and I have come to be laid along with him.

(*Bucket and Snagsby assist him to the gate. Jo gets in Picture on the steps, looking through the gate. Snagsby and Bucket leave him, but stand close at hand.*)

Buc. I can't bear this.

Snags. Nor I.

(*Jo comes down a little, C, speaking to them, dreamily.*)

Jo. You'll have to get the key of the gate to let me in, for it's allays locked.

(*Tries to return, but falls weak and staggers. They catch him in their arms, and kneel with him, and bring him down, C.*)

Jo. It's turned wery dark. Is there any light comin'?

Snags. It's coming fast, Jo. Jo, my poor fellow!

Jo. I can hear you, sir, in the dark; but I'm gropin'—a-gropin'. Let me catch hold of your hand.

Snags. Jo, can you hear what I say?

Jo. I'll hear anything as you say, for I knows it's good.

Snags. (*In a whisper.*) Our Father,

Jo. (*Faintly.*) Our Father,

Snags. Which art in Heaven,

Jo. Which art in Heaven,

Snags. Hallowed be thy name.

Jo. Hallowed be thy name. (*Dies.*)

SLOW CURTAIN.

Printed by Libri Plureos GmbH in Hamburg, Germany